GENERATIVE AI
in the
COURTROOM

A PRACTICAL HANDBOOK FOR MODERN JUSTICE

"EMPOWERING INDIA'S LEGAL PROFESSIONALS WITH AI TOOLS AND TECHNIQUES"

ASPIRE K SWAMINATHAN
ANITA THOMAS

ISBN
Paperback 979-8-89556-604-6
Hardcase 979-8-89588-272-6

Contents

SECTION A: CHAPTERS

1. **Understanding Generative AI in Law** 27

This chapter introduces the fundamental concepts of Generative AI and its applications in the legal domain. It explores how AI is reshaping legal research, document drafting, and judicial decision-making.

A look at the pressing challenges faced by the Indian judiciary, including case backlogs, slow processes, and inefficiencies. This chapter discusses where AI can step in to streamline and optimize these processes.

This chapter delves into how AI tools are transforming traditional legal research. It compares AI-driven legal research platforms with conventional methods, highlighting their advantages and applications.

Exploring the use of AI to enhance courtroom procedures, this chapter covers automation of administrative tasks, case management, real-time legal assistance, and evidence organization.

A guide on how AI can be used to draft contracts, pleadings, and other legal documents. This chapter demonstrates how AI reduces manual errors, accelerates drafting time, and improves accuracy.

10. Full Spectrum Roadmap for Integration of AI into Indian Judiciary. . . 151

A detailed roadmap for AI adoption in the Indian judiciary, covering policy, infrastructure, training, and stakeholder engagement, drawing lessons from previous technological initiatives like e-Courts.

11. The Future of AI in the Indian Judiciary 165

A forward-looking chapter that analyzes emerging trends in AI technology, including predictive analytics, virtual courtrooms, and the integration of AI with blockchain and other technologies.

12. Data Privacy in Legal AI – Myths, Realities, and the Path to Adoption. 177

This chapter addresses common concerns regarding data privacy in AI, debunking myths and offering practical solutions for ensuring the security of sensitive legal data in AI-driven platforms.

SECTION B: CASE STUDIES

Foreword

I take great pride in presenting "Generative AI in the Courtroom: A Handbook for the Indian Judiciary," a book that arrives at a crucial juncture, providing timely insights into the intersection of AI and law. On August 12, 2024, the Supreme Court confirmed the use of AI in legal research and translation. A total of 36,271 judgments into Hindi and 17,142 translations into 16 other regional languages were effected using AI. The Supreme Court of India implemented the National Policy and Action Plan for ICT deployment in the Indian Judiciary (Action Plan 2005) via the e-Courts Project 2005. Since then, we have made significant strides, bringing about transformation both gradually and decisively, a testament to our commitment and progress in the Indian Judiciary.

In 2018, I had the opportunity to humbly serve the AI Task Force set up by the Ministry of Commerce and Industry and, as Chairman, submit a report. In this report, we settled the boggling question about AI. We remarked AI as *"the Science and Engineering of making intelligent machines, brilliant computer programs", with 'intelligence' being "the computational part of the ability to achieve goals in the world and brilliance is the ability to create transformative and adaptive use cases"*. Following this, we simplified the explanation of AI's grand purpose. This was in perfect relation to a similar task of using computers to understand or mimic human intelligence. We remarked that the intelligence part need not have to confine itself to methods that are biologically observable. This report also outlined the grand challenges of AI and its relevance to our nation. We also drew attention to the responsible use of AI, emphasizing ethics, social safety, legal framework, etc. We recommended that AI be seen as a *"Scalable Problem Solver and not just booster of economic growth"* and stressed ethical considerations in AI implementation. These reports, along with other studies by the GOI, have conclusively demonstrated the transformative potential of AI in governance and administration. The success of e-governance and digital governance models in our nation is a promising indicator of the potential of AI.

I must admit that I initially planned to focus on the aspects of this book relevant to me as a computer scientist. Also, since I serve the GOI in many techno-policy-related aspects, I planned to focus only on these. However, as I glanced through, I realised I was drawn to the compelling narrative aspects and thus began engrossed in them. This short book vividly narrates the impact of adopting AI and, therefore, the transformative effect it would bring to the efficiency and effectiveness of our judicial system.

It is necessary to stress here that adopting generative AI means that it can create new content rather than doing very generic and specific tasks. This aspect makes it more exciting and challenging. Our judicial system has acknowledged many challenges, to list a few: the backlog of cases, fair and equitable access to judiciary services, speedy case resolution, and catering to ethnic and regional diversity have been exponentially growing.

This book addresses these challenges and does not just discuss AI as some futuristic fancy technology. It explains AI and Generative AI and their compelling and non-deniable relevance by breaking down and explaining how lawyers, judges, and court administrators can adopt and deploy them to make work efficient, reliable, and fair. This approach is very practical, particularly emphasising the need to maintain the human element of justice while embracing AI technology. This book further makes me appreciate two aspects, ethics and values, that must accompany any such introduction of AI into the judiciary and a case for how AI may serve as an assistant to humans rather than replace them in the judicial process while ensuring the fairness and transparency that resonate at the heart of our legal system. We technologists otherwise call it ethical, explainable, and responsible AI in terms of measurable processes and metrics.

I opine that this book will serve as a much-needed resource for legal professionals and spawn a future conversation on the role AI can and must play in shaping the judiciary in India's future. Thus, this book has become quite timely in contributing to the national AI discourse. My hope is that it may also inspire many more stakeholders to pursue possibilities ahead. To me, the authors have fairly represented the efforts involved in putting together such an important work; they bring a welcome and critical step forward to bridging technology and the legal profession. I wish the readers the best as they advance and discover AI and its indispensable relevance to our judicial system and stakeholders.

Warm regards,

Prof. V. Kamakoti

Director, IIT Madras

Preface:
The Story Behind This Book

The seeds of this book were sown when the inspiration for a key insight fell upon me as I listened to the Chief Justice of India D.Y. Chandrachud deliver the keynote address at the Indo-Singapore Judicial Conference earlier this year. While passionately appealing for the ethical integration of AI into the Indian judiciary, Chief Justice Chandrachud explained how AI can completely change the face of the existing judicial system, especially with respect to facilitation of legal research and judicial processes. This is what touched my heart and thus motivated me to write this book.

Chief Justice Chandrachud's call for AI is not a mere call for development in technology but a deep recognition of the needs of our evolving legal system. The address underlined the responsible use of AI, viewing the integration of this technology into the judiciary as one that upholds the values of fairness, transparency, and equity. His vision provided the catalyst for exploring how Generative AI might be both effectively and ethically integrated into the Indian Judiciary. I have seen the transformational role of technologies in reordering businesses, institutions, and processes from very close quarters. My work has been quite diversified-from being among the early pioneers of AI and technology strategy in the corporate world to being an adviser to political campaigns and governance initiatives in India. This experience gave me a ringside view and a rather profound understanding of how data & technology, when well-harnessed, can help solve some of the most deep-seated challenges. These experiences, along with the felt need expressed by Chief Justice Chandrachud, created a melting point that gave birth to this book. As a Research Scholar in the Doctorate Degree course on Generative AI, I have been researching ways in which this latest technology can bring about radical changes in many fields, including law. Its peculiar uniqueness, with complexities and scale, makes it mired in a special set of problems-massive backlogs, inordinate delays in procedure, barriers to accessibility-which could, with the proper interventions of technology, be overcome. But as the Chief Justice aptly noted, this is not a journey about mere introductions of technologies; it is to make sure these tools are thoughtfully and ethically fitted into our judiciary.

The book is designed as a helpful guide for judges, lawyers, court administrators, and even policymakers in general. The goal here is not just to grasp what Generative AI is, but most importantly to have practical tools and techniques that could really be put into place in daily operations with a view to make justice quicker, more straightforward, and more accessible. The inspiration for the book also comes from the deep involvement I have with the tech space, not only in business but also in politics and governance. Having set up the IT wing of a major political party in India, having contributed to the tech-enabled election strategies, I have been a personal witness to how data and technology can bring about effective change. Although that would be a correct statement, as I am neither a practicing lawyer nor formally trained in the field of law, I strongly believe that my somewhat rare perspective and experience with the intersection of technology, business, politics, and governance afford me a valid and beneficial vantage point from which to begin exploring this integration of Generative AI within the judiciary.

I have in the last few months held quite a number of in-depth discussions with lawyers who are practitioners of their craft, as well as sitting judges and learned scholars in the field of law, all of whom have shared their various insights and experiences on the current challenges facing the judiciary. These conversations served as a very good reference to understand the workflows, bottlenecks, and practical realities of the legal ecosystem. My work has always been driven by an urge to find innovative solutions to complex problems, and through that lens is how I approach the subject of AI in the Judiciary.

This book is a culmination of collaboration with legal experts and my own research as a scholar in Generative AI. By trying to bridge the gap between technology and law, I aspired to contribute meaningfully to the ongoing discourse of how we can make justice more accessible, efficient, and fair. I did not try to replace nuanced expert opinion by legal practitioners but put forward a different point of view on how AI can be ethically and effectively used in courts to help solve some of the most important challenges the judiciary faces.

Writing this book, I hope to put in my mite to keep talking about what the Indian judiciary would be and what role AI can play in shaping that future. I invite you, dear reader, to share this journey with me as I engage with arguments on how we can use Generative AI to take our judiciary forward and make it far more responsive to the aspirations of all those it will serve. This book, however, is not a mere theory, but more of a call to action for all of us who have thrown our energies into the vortex of human affairs and have committed ourselves to ensuring that the promise of justice is not a distant ideal but a living reality in the lives of each and every citizen.

Its genesis perhaps lay in a book of foresight; the insight of Chief Justice Chandrachud at the Indo-Singapore Judicial Conference that integration of AI into the judiciary is at its very core not about technological advance but about bringing into reality through the wisdom of our judicial leaders propelled by the best that modern technology could offer a dream of access to justice for all.

A Word of Thanks

Completing this book has been a journey of collaboration, learning, and discovery, and it would not have been possible without the support and contributions of many incredible people.

First and foremost, I would like to extend my heartfelt gratitude to my family for their unwavering support throughout the journey of writing this book. A special mention goes to my wife, **Pavithra** whose constant encouragement and patience have been a pillar of strength, and to my daughters, **Maya and Ananya**, who graciously helped with proofreading and provided invaluable encouragement along the way. Your belief in my work and understanding made this project possible, and I am forever grateful.

A special acknowledgment goes to **Mr. Nizamuddin**, a **retired Superintendent of Police** and a close friend, philosopher, and guide. Beyond being a fine human being, Mr. Nizamuddin is a respected and thorough professional in many areas, having earned immense respect throughout his 35 years of service in law enforcement. His deep knowledge and experience in law and order, crime, and his numerous interactions with courts, lawyers, and judges across all levels of the judiciary provided invaluable insights for this book. His inputs helped me understand the systemic challenges facing the judiciary today, from practical on-the-ground issues to high-level legal complexities.

Mr. Nizamuddin was always available, offering his guidance and wisdom whenever needed, regardless of the time or situation. His commitment to sharing his experiences and perspectives enriched this work, giving me the clarity and real-world perspectives I needed to truly capture the current state of our legal system. His influence on this book has been immeasurable, and I am deeply grateful for his support throughout this journey.

I would also like to thank my **friends** and colleagues who provided invaluable feedback and guidance. Many conversations with you helped shape the direction of this book, offering fresh perspectives and insights that improved its content.

A special acknowledgment to the **lawyers and retired judges** who lent their expertise, shared their experiences, and critically examined the ideas presented. Your firsthand knowledge of the judicial system added depth and authenticity to this work, ensuring that it is both relevant and practical.

I am particularly grateful to my **co-author, Ms. Anita Thomas**, whose contribution was indispensable. As a practicing lawyer, Anita tirelessly reviewed every legal aspect of this book to ensure accuracy and precision. Her deep understanding of law and her commitment to this project made sure that everything stood the test of legal scrutiny. Thank you, Anita, for your partnership, dedication, and friendship throughout this endeavor.

And now, for a light-hearted yet sincere note of thanks to **ChatGPT and other Generative AI tools**, which, despite having no emotions or coffee breaks, played an unexpected but crucial role in structuring, organizing, and compiling this book. Whether it was assisting in drafting, fine-tuning ideas, or suggesting references, AI became my co-pilot in getting through the more repetitive aspects of writing. You've saved me countless hours—and the inevitable *headaches*—that come with structuring long-form content. So here's a special mention to my ever-available digital assistant, always ready to brainstorm at 2 AM when human editors are understandably sleeping!

Finally, to all the **readers and future practitioners** of AI-driven legal solutions, this book is for you. I hope it inspires new ways of thinking about the law, the judiciary, and the potential of technology in transforming the delivery of justice.

With gratitude,

Aspire K Swaminathan

A Note from the Co-Author, *Anita Thomas*

As someone who has been practicing law for over 30 years, spanning civil, company law, and maritime matters across various courts, I have had the privilege of seeing the legal ecosystem from multiple angles. However, there have also been moments of deep frustration—delays that seem never-ending, cases that drag on despite the best efforts of diligent lawyers, judges, and court staff. The sheer volume of work and the inefficiencies built into the system often leave both legal professionals and litigants feeling powerless, despite our collective dedication to justice.

It was during one of these reflective moments, about six months ago, when Swaminathan reached out to discuss an idea that immediately piqued my interest. He proposed using **Generative AI** as a tool to address some of the inefficiencies and delays we've all come to accept as part of the legal process. His vision wasn't just to make the judiciary faster or more efficient, but to truly **transform** the way justice is delivered—making it more accessible, equitable, and transparent.

I remember feeling a sense of hope as we talked. It was exciting to imagine how the legal ecosystem as we know it could change. Co-authoring this book was my way of giving back to the system that has shaped me, by contributing something that could ease the burden on the system and allow legal professionals to focus on what truly matters: the delivery of justice.

This book is our way of offering a practical roadmap for the integration of AI into the judiciary. It's not just about technology for technology's sake, but about making meaningful changes that can help alleviate some of the frustrations many of us have felt throughout our careers. My hope is that through this work, we can help usher in a future where justice is not only delivered but delivered **efficiently and fairly**—because we know that justice delayed is justice denied.

- **Anita Thomas**

Introduction

The world over, at the height of ruthless metamorphosis and with technology redefining almost all aspects of our lives, the legal profession is standing at one of its most critical crossroads. Thus, the judiciary, meant to be a bedrock of any democratic way of life, finds itself with unparalleled pressure to dispense justice with more speed, fairness, and transparency than ever.

Whereas in the traditional approach, methods lag behind at a time when the burden of cases keeps rising and demands on the dispensation of legal services are getting more and more complex.

Recently, Chief Justice of India D.Y. Chandrachud brought to light a very important fact-that the judiciary is there to serve the citizens and the judiciary must change to serve them better. The clarion call stirs an important need for innovation within our legal system. The question today is not whether technology will change the judiciary, but how we can ensure it does so in a manner that furthers the ends of justice and equity.

This book is a direct response to that challenge. Having spent years at the intersection of technology, business, and governance, I have watched the transformational power of innovation up close. My journey-from being one of the pioneers of AI strategies in the corporate world, to advising political campaigns and participating in governance has provided a privileged insight into how technology can be used as a force for good, especially in those very areas where it is needed most.

Why This Book? Why Now?

We are just on the cusp of this new era, and it is clear that generative-AI is much more than simply an efficiency tool, serving merely as a catalyst to transformation. That may mean automation of routine tasks, developing legal research, increasing access to justice, and even supporting judges with decision-making in their courts. As great as the potential of Generative AI is to meet systemic challenges in our judiciaries, this integration into practice will need thoughtful consideration, ethical framing, and an implementation strategy.

This book couldn't have come at a better time. Along with the advancement in Generative AI technology, it is high time that the legal fraternity opens its arms wide to receive the benefits and is aware of the lurking challenges. This is not just a book about technology; this is a book about where law and innovation meet at a time when the stakes have never been so high.

For Whom?

This book targets a wide audience involved in the legal ecosystem: judges, lawyers, court administrators, and policy makers, among others from academia. Whether a professional well-seasoned or just entering into this field, this book will bring value about how Generative AI can be integrated into your work. In fact, this should be a helpful working guide for those who work to modernize the judiciary in such a way as to keep it sensitive to the needs of those it serves.

What This Book Is

"Generative AI in the Courtroom: A Practical Handbook for Modern Justice" is an empirical guide in understanding and implementing Generative AI in the legal field. Designed not only to educate but to provide hands-on tools and techniques within the context of everyday practice, each chapter offers a how-to guide, examples of real-life examples, and case studies showing how AI makes the tangential difference in justice delivery. This book is for the legal initiate preparing to don the cloak of the future. It is a road map as to how AI may be deployed into the judicial process-a process that, quite bluntly, must enhance efficiency, accuracy, and access to justice with no diminution of the integrity of our legal system.

What This Book Is NOT

This is not a technical book replete with buzzwords and complicated algorithms. One will have a good understanding of how Generative AI actually works, but it is more practical in application than deep into technical aspects. You really do not need to be a techie in order to understand this book; all you need is an open mindset to learn how technology can support and augment your work. This is not a book designed to offer one-size-fits-all solutions for the many challenges faced by the judiciary, but rather an enabling framework and set of tools that can be adapted for concrete legal contexts. This work inspires experimentation, critical thinking, and ethical consideration rather than dictating fixed rules or solutions.

The Road Ahead

As we embark on this journey together, let me invite you to the exploration of the possibilities that Generative AI has in offering. This book is not about learning new technologies but how we reimagine justice delivery in a rapidly changing world. It's about how we make sure our judiciary is strong, resilient, and above all, just.

Welcome to the future of law-a future where technology supports and extends, rather than supplants, human judgment in an effort to achieve a more effective, fair, and available legal system for all.

Section A:
Chapters

CHAPTER ONE: UNDERSTANDING GENERATIVE AI IN LAW
THE ROLE OF AI IN MODERNIZING THE JUDICIARY

Vignette: The Day the System Changed

In a small district court in Kerala, Judge Arun sat staring at the piles of case files that had accumulated on his desk over the past few weeks. The district had seen a sharp increase in petty theft cases, and with each passing day, the backlog grew. Despite working late into the night, there seemed to be no end in sight. He was just one judge among hundreds across the country, each battling similar backlogs in their own jurisdictions.

But today was different. Today, a new tool was being introduced—a tool that promised to change the way justice was delivered. As Judge Arun opened the AI-assisted case management system on his computer, he couldn't help but feel a mixture of skepticism and hope. Could a machine really help reduce the burden on the judiciary? Could it assist in delivering justice more swiftly and accurately?

He clicked on a case file, and the AI immediately began analyzing the details, cross-referencing it with past judgments, and highlighting the most relevant precedents. In minutes, the AI provided a summary that would have taken Arun hours to compile. For the first time in weeks, he felt like he could see the light at the end of the tunnel. The system wasn't making decisions for him—it was empowering him to make better, faster decisions.

As he moved on to the next file, a thought crossed his mind: perhaps today was the day the system truly began to change. The day when the scales of justice, long weighed down by inefficiency, began to balance once more.

Understanding Generative AI in Law

This chapter introduces the fundamental concepts of Generative AI and its applications in the legal domain. It explores how AI is reshaping legal research, document drafting, and judicial decision-making.

Welcome to the first step on your journey into the world of Generative AI in the legal system. If you've picked up this book, chances are you're curious about how technology can make your life easier in the courtroom, your office, or perhaps in managing legal research. The good news? You're in the right place. Let's start by demystifying this term that's been buzzing around—Generative AI—and why it's not just a futuristic concept, but something you can actually start using today.

What is Generative AI?

Generative AI might sound like something out of a sci-fi movie, but it's actually a lot simpler than it seems. In the broadest sense, AI, or Artificial Intelligence, refers to computer systems that can perform tasks that usually require human intelligence. This includes things like recognizing speech, making decisions, or even understanding natural language.

Now, Generative AI takes this one step further. Instead of just analyzing existing information, Generative AI can create new content—think of it like a very smart assistant who not only understands your requests but can also draft a legal brief, summarize a lengthy document, or even generate predictive insights based on patterns it has learned. Imagine telling your AI tool, "Draft a motion based on these case details," and within minutes, you have a first draft ready for review. That's the power of Generative AI.

Why Generative AI Matters in Law

You might be wondering, "Why should I care about Generative AI? I've been practicing law just fine without it." And that's a fair point. But here's the thing—**Generative AI isn't here to replace you; it's here to enhance what you do.**

Think about the time you spend on repetitive tasks—reviewing documents, drafting similar contracts over and over, or sifting through mountains of case law to find that one precedent that could make or break your case. What if you could cut that time in half? What if, instead of spending hours on research, you could focus on strategy, on the things that truly require your expertise? That's where Generative AI comes in.

Automating the mundane means that it frees you up to focus on what really matters, which is fashioning arguments, advising clients, and seeing that justice is served. This is not about making you redundant but making you more efficient and effective, hence more successful.

Generative AI in Action: A Glimpse from Other Industries

To fully appreciate the potential of Generative AI in law, it helps to first review how it's already been transforming other industries. Take healthcare, for example. Doctors are using AI to diagnose diseases with unprecedented precision; their programs catch issues that might pass even the most trained human eye. In finance, AI makes prediction about market trends, enabling investors to make wiser decisions faster.

It is no different for the legal field. Just as AI can help a doctor save lives, it can help you save time, keep off mistakes, and better serve your clients. The parallels are striking, and the possibilities are endless.

The Evolution of AI in Law

Before we dive deep into Generative AI, it is worth stepping back and viewing how AI has evolved in the legal field. You likely have already begun using some of the tools which leverage AI for simple, routine tasks: document review software that automatically underlines relevant clauses, case management systems that keep you on top of deadlines.

While that is vastly useful, the leap will come with Generative AI. It's no more about analyzing data; it's about creating new content, first drafts, and insights that might take so much more time for humans to develop. We're moving, as it were, from reactive to proactive technology: AI that doesn't just respond to your commands but anticipates your needs and assists you in ways you may not even expect.

Challenges in the Implementation of AI in Law Admittedly, integrating any new technology has its share of challenges, and Generative AI makes no exception. Among the very biggest is the sheer complexity of legal language. For example, training AI in legal jargon, context, and the minutiae of law that might vary significantly from one jurisdiction to another takes a lot of time.

Then, there is the issue of data privacy. The whole legal profession is built on confidentiality, and this will require you to believe whatever input you give to AI will be safe from possible data breaches. Fortunately, many of these AI tools are designed with that in mind, with added layers for encryption and security that keep sensitive information safe.

Other challenges include the one on bias: the AI learns from the data given, and if that data is biased, the output of the AI can be, too. This is particularly concerning in legal contexts where biased decisions can carry serious consequences. The key is in using AI tools that are transparent about their data sources and how they process information.

These, however, are not insurmountable challenges. Choosing the right set of tools and using them judiciously could minimize these risks while gaining the advantages of Generative AI.

Getting Started with Generative AI: Tools at Your Disposal

Now for the fun stuff-how you might actually get started applying Generative AI in your practice. There are some tools out there designed just for legal professionals, and the best part is that you do not have to be a technophile to use them.

- **GPT-4:** This is one of the most developed kinds of generative AI out in the market today. It helps with the drafting of documents, summarizing long texts, and can even create content with prompts given. You might need a 100-page contract summarized for you in minutes.

- **LegalMation:** Probably the most relevant for document automation, you input the case information, and it will spit out drafts of pleadings, discovery responses, and other legal documents, thus saving hours of work.

- **ROSS Intelligence:** Though its main focus is on legal research, ROSS uses AI to understand your questions and return highly relevant answers from legal databases.

Intuitive tools require minimal training for immediate use. They are to augment your capability, not replace you-think of these tools as an extension of your capability that will afford you the freedom to work on the areas of the law that call for your unique human touch.

These are just a few popular tools globally that demonstrate the potential of AI in the legal space. It's important to note that new tools are being developed and introduced into the market every day, each tailored to different aspects of legal practice. In India, several AI-driven tools are gaining traction, designed specifically for the nuances of the Indian legal system.

- **CaseMine:** An Indian AI-powered legal research tool offering intelligent case law analysis. It helps lawyers generate contextually relevant cases and develop case strategies more effectively. Its strength lies in sifting through Indian judicial precedents and providing insights highly applicable to local legal contexts.

- **NearLaw:** This platform enables Indian legal professionals to access judgments, citations, and court orders quickly. NearLaw offers analytical features to help better understand Indian legal documents and case law.

- **Manupatra:** A well-established legal research tool in India, Manupatra incorporates AI for predictive analysis, document comparison, and case law recommendations. It is well-known for its comprehensive database of Indian laws, statutes, and judgments, tailored specifically for Indian legal practices.

In addition to these, platforms like **Adalat.ai** and **LawSimpl.ai** are emerging as powerful AI tools for the Indian legal ecosystem:

- **Adalat.ai:** A platform that focuses on **document automation** and **contract review**, enabling Indian legal professionals to streamline the review and drafting of complex legal documents, significantly reducing manual work.

- **LawSimpl.ai:** Designed to simplify legal processes for both individuals and law firms, this platform offers **legal drafting, contract generation, and research support**. LawSimpl.ai seeks to bridge the gap between technology and law, making high-volume document review and case preparation faster and more efficient.

Together, these tools demonstrate how AI is evolving to support the specific needs of Indian legal professionals. As the legal AI landscape continues to expand, practitioners can expect more innovative tools designed to streamline their work and enhance productivity, making AI an invaluable asset for modern law practices in India.

A New Era of Legal Practice

As we end this first chapter, let us not forget: the practice of law has never been about the rules and procedure alone. It is about people, it is about justice, and making a difference to the world. Generative AI will not change that; it will enhance it.

By adopting these innovative tools, you will position yourself to deliver better, faster, and more reliable outcomes for your clients. You are embracing a future in which technology and human expertise go hand in hand, each making the other stronger.

As you read through the following pages, keep your mind open. Experiment with these tools; see what works for you, and do not be afraid to push the boundaries of what is possible. The generative AI is not only the future of law but the present to guide you through success.

Questions for Reflection

1. **AI's Impact on Justice Delivery:**

   How do you think AI can transform the way justice is delivered in India? What are the potential benefits and pitfalls?

   ____

   ____

   ____

   ____

   ____

   ____

   In what ways might AI challenge the traditional roles of judges, lawyers, and court administrators?

   ____

   ____

   ____

   ____

   ____

   ____

2. **Accessibility and Equity:**

Can AI truly make the judicial system more accessible to the underprivileged and marginalized communities? What are the potential barriers to this?

____

____

____

____

____

____

____

How can AI help bridge the gap between urban and rural access to justice in India?

____

____

____

____

____

____

____

3. **Challenges in Implementation:**

What are the biggest challenges in implementing AI in the judiciary? How can these challenges be overcome?

____

____

____

____

____

____

How do you foresee resistance from legal professionals being addressed when integrating AI into the legal system?

____

____

____

____

____

____

____

Scenario for Debate

Imagine a scenario where a fully AI-powered court is introduced in a pilot project, handling cases autonomously with minimal human intervention.

- **Debate Topic:** Should this model be expanded to more courts, or should the human element remain central to judicial proceedings? Discuss the implications for justice, accountability, and public trust.

Hands-On Exercise

Research and list out the AI tools currently being used in judicial systems around the world. Compare their functionalities and outcomes with those of traditional court systems. Reflect on how these tools could be adapted for the Indian judiciary.

CHAPTER TWO: MAPPING THE CHALLENGES - WHERE AI CAN MAKE A DIFFERENCE

Vignette: The Overwhelmed Public Prosecutor

In the bustling city of Mumbai, Arvind, a senior public prosecutor, sat at his desk, surrounded by towering stacks of case files. His role required him to juggle multiple high-profile cases simultaneously, each with complex details, witness testimonies, and legal precedents to review. Despite his vast experience, Arvind found himself struggling to keep up with the sheer volume of cases and the pressure to deliver timely justice.

One particular case—a fraud involving a web of financial transactions—had been dragging on for months. Sifting through thousands of pages of documents, reviewing contracts, and cross-referencing legal statutes was an overwhelming task. He worked late into the night, trying to ensure no important detail was missed.

During a legal conference, Arvind was introduced to the potential of AI tools in managing caseloads and automating document analysis. At first, he was skeptical. How could a machine understand the complexities of legal documents? But as the backlog in his office grew, he decided to give it a try.

Within a week of implementing an AI-driven legal research tool, the results were astonishing. The AI combed through massive amounts of data, summarizing key points and identifying critical patterns in financial records—tasks that would have taken Arvind days to complete on his own. The system even flagged similar cases with legal precedents that helped him strengthen his arguments. Arvind's team experienced newfound efficiency, allowing them to focus on the strategic aspects of their work.

For the first time in months, Arvind felt he was no longer buried under paperwork. AI wasn't replacing him—it was giving him the time and clarity to focus on what truly mattered: delivering justice.

Mapping the Challenges – Where AI Can Make a Difference

A look at the pressing challenges faced by the Indian judiciary, including case backlogs, slow processes, and inefficiencies. This chapter discusses where AI can step in to streamline and optimize these processes.

The challenges are as old as the system itself in the world of the judiciary, which is very vast and intricate. Delays, inconsistencies, and access issues have plagued the courts for decades. But with every challenge comes an opportunity-an opportunity to rethink, reimagine, and innovate. This chapter shall identify those challenges within the Indian judiciary and find out how far the Generative AI provides the solutions we desperately need today.

Current Status: Entailing the Problem

The Indian judiciary, be it in scale or operation, has often been described as a behemoth that, in ways, has over time grown into a guardian of justice. Besides their importance, the system is bogged down by several persistent challenges:

1. **Large number of pending cases**: A big problem in the present day is of pending cases. More than 40 million cases are pending in different courts in India as of 2023, while in some of these cases, their hearing started decades ago. This is not just a backlog of mere numbers but represents real people who wait for justice, with their lives held up due to various unnecessary delays.

2. **Incoherent Decisions**: Another challenge that comes along with the inconsistency of the rulings by the various courts is that this inconsistency could give the perception of great unpredictability and, in some instances, perceived unfairness.

3. **Access to Justice**: Most view the legal system as an intimidating, costly, inaccessible entity. Most judicial language is obscure and inhibits ordinary people's access to the very system designed for their protection.

4. **Procedural Delays**: Procedural delays are another major issue arising from administrative inefficiency. Certain simple tasks, like fixing cases for hearing or filing of documents, or even internal communications within the different departments of the court, get laboriously drawn out beyond any semblance of reason.

All these problems have a snowballing effect, from the concerned individuals to society in general. A justice system that is unable to deliver timely and consistent results cannot possibly retain the confidence of the people it serves.

How Generative AI Can Make a Difference

Now, exactly how can Generative AI step in to beat these conditions? Okay, let's break them down one at a time.

1. **Ease Case Backlogs with AI-Powered Case Management**
   - **Current Scenario**: In the traditional scenario, management of case files is quite a laborious process. Every case is marked by mountains of paper, countless numbers of hearings, and intricate details that must be followed closely. The process is manual in nature; hence, the cases get delayed for reasons as redundant as administrative bottlenecks.
   - **How AI Can Help**: It's where generative AI now comes in, making the difference in case management. By automating routine tasks such as document filing, case scheduling, and deadline tracking, for example, AI can significantly cut down the time needed to process a case through the system. Other AI-powered tools actually triage cases by priority to make sure critical ones go first.
   - **Example:** All documents are automatically put into order by a case management system; it even schedules hearings with the help of AI. Potential delays based on past patterns will also be predicted by the AI. CaseMine and ROSS Intelligence can sift through the case law and put together summaries and relevant precedents in a fraction of the time a human would take.

- ○ **Hands-on Learning**: If you are a legal professional, use a tool like CaseMine for maintaining a small set of cases. Observe how AI handles the organization of files, suggests relevant precedents, and keeps track of deadlines. You will notice that you'll free up a lot of time spent on administrative tasks and would be able to work more on strategy and client interaction.

2. **Bringing Consistency in Rulings**

- ○ **Present Situation**: The inconsistency in the verdicts is a big problem; specifically, the ones that come from lower courts probably face limitations to comprehensive legal databases and facilities. The judges have different support and means to bring about different conclusions to similar cases.

- ○ **How AI Can Help**: AI can also help analyze enormous volumes of legal data and identify patterns and precedents so that judgments are more consistent. If AI-generated summaries and analyses of relevant case law are provided for judges, then the possibilities of divergent decisions would be minimal.

  For example, something like LexisNexis or Jurisprudence Analytics could be employed. They would analyze case law from other jurisdictions, what the rulings on similar cases have been elsewhere, and provide that in a comprehensive report to the judges. It does not replace the decision-making process of the judge himself. Rather, with the help of data insights, the process is enhanced.

- ○ **Hands-on Learning Activity**: As a judge or legal researcher, use LexisNexis to understand how AI can help in identifying consistent patterns in case law. Run a search in the case type of your choice and compare the AI-driven insights against your own research. You would notice that AI is indeed a very good second opinion that helps you make well-informed decisions with consistency in view of legal precedents.

3. **Improving Access to Justice**

   o **Current Status**: Inaccessibility of the judicial system has become a tough task for many citizens, especially rural people. Firstly, the legal services are highly expensive and the process of law is highly complicated to such an extent that a person without proper education and knowledge about the laws cannot handle the situation on their own.

   o **How AI Can Help**: Democratization of access to legal information can be facilitated by AI-navigated chatbots and virtual legal assistants. These will have potential for imparting primary legal advice, understanding legal documents, and even guiding someone through the filing of a case without expensive legal representation.

   o For instance, tools like DoNotPay have already started changing the legal landscape. What started as a "robot lawyer" that fought parking tickets has grown to cover everything from small claims to consumer rights. By the use of its simple chat interface, users can interact with the AI and get tailor-made advice without necessarily having to see a lawyer.

   o **Hands-on Learning**: If you're the legal aid provider or a community working with the law, try to develop an AI chatbot using resources like ChatGPT. Use it to program responses to simple legal questions that clients frequently ask. You'll get to appreciate how AI will help bridge the gap between citizens and the legal system for accessible justice to all.

4. **Quicker Court Procedures**

   o **Current Situation**: Administration is one of the bigger reasons for case backlogs, with inefficiency oozing from the scheduling of hearings to the filing of documents and inter-departmental communication within a court.

   o **How AI Can Help**: AI can automate many of these, ensuring speed and accuracy. From automatic document generation to AI-assisted scheduling, the potential for reducing procedural delays is huge.

Example: AI-powered applications are already being used in some jurisdictions to generate legal documents on standard templates. For instance, LegalMation proposes lawyers write complaints, motions, and a lot of other documents within minutes, just by entering the case details in question. Similarly, the scheduling system powered by AI can easily undertake the work of allotting court dates automatically, without much backward and forward correspondence.

- o **Hands-on Learning**: Use LegalMation to prepare a standard legal document such as a motion or a contract. Compare the AI-created version with one you would create manually. Note the time it would save, and reflect on how that time savings would free up resources to be used to make additional progress toward decreasing court system delays.

A Future-Ready Judiciary

The problems besetting the Indian judiciary are enormous, but they are not insurmountable. Embracing Generative AI would go a long way in tackling these problems head-on for a system that is not only more efficient but also more just.

As we move on to explore AI in the legal areas of practice, remember, it is not to take the place of human judgment but to improve it. AI is a tool, and by using it judiciously, it will help us create a judiciary serving the people, as envisioned by Chief Justice Chandrachud.

Take, therefore, some time to play with the tools presented in this chapter. Muster a fit for your practice and begin considering how you can be part of the transformation that the judiciary so desperately needs. The future of justice is less about more laws or more courts, but more about wiser and more functional systems leveraging from the best of what technology has to offer.

Questions for Reflection:

1. **What are the biggest challenges currently facing the Indian judiciary that hinder the timely delivery of justice?**

   Reflect on how these challenges impact not just legal professionals but also the public's trust in the system.

   ____

   ____

   ____

   ____

   ____

   ____

   ____

2. **How do you think AI could help address the issue of case backlogs and reduce the burden on legal professionals?**

   Consider specific examples from your experience where AI could streamline processes.

   ____

   ____

   ____

   ____

   ____

   ____

3. **What are some areas in your legal practice where time-consuming, repetitive tasks could be automated with the help of AI?**

Think about how automation could free up more time for higher-value tasks.

____

____

____

____

____

____

____

4. **Why do you think some legal professionals are hesitant to adopt AI despite the clear benefits in terms of efficiency?**

Reflect on whether these concerns are valid and how they could be addressed.

____

____

____

____

____

____

____

Scenarios for Debate:

1. **Scenario**: A law firm dealing with thousands of ongoing cases is considering adopting AI tools to manage document review and case prioritization. However, senior partners worry that the introduction of AI may lead to a reduction in jobs and loss of human oversight.

   Debate: Should the firm move forward with AI adoption despite these concerns? How can they balance efficiency gains with ethical considerations regarding job displacement?

2. **Scenario**: A government public defender's office is struggling to keep up with an overwhelming number of cases. An AI-powered solution promises to help them handle the administrative load, but the office's limited budget and the perceived complexity of implementing AI make them hesitant.

   Debate: Is the investment in AI worth it for a government office operating on limited funds? How can the benefits of AI outweigh the initial cost and complexity of integration?

3. **Scenario**: A judge handling a complex fraud case is inundated with technical financial details that are beyond their expertise. The court has access to AI-driven analytical tools that can process financial data, but the judge is unsure whether to rely on them for fear of making a decision based on AI analysis.

Debate: Should the judge incorporate AI assistance in processing data? How can human oversight and AI work together in cases that require specialized knowledge?

CHAPTER THREE: INDISPENSABLE AI TOOLS FOR LEGAL RESEARCH AND CASE MANAGEMENT

AI IN LEGAL RESEARCH AND DATA MANAGEMENT

Vignette: The Hunt for Precedent

Meera was a young associate at a bustling law firm in Mumbai, where the pressure to find the right legal precedents for her cases was immense. Her latest assignment involved researching a complicated case about intellectual property rights, with a tight deadline looming over her head. The firm's library, once the heart of legal research, now seemed more like a relic of the past—too slow and too cumbersome to meet the demands of modern legal practice.

This time, though, she had a secret weapon: an AI-powered legal research tool that had been recently integrated into the firm's operations. Dubbed "Lexi," the AI was designed to sift through thousands of legal documents, judgments, and statutes at lightning speed.

Skeptical but desperate, Meera uploaded the case details into Lexi. Within moments, the screen populated with a curated list of relevant precedents, complete with summaries and contextual notes. It even suggested legal strategies based on similar cases from the past decade. What would have taken Meera hours, or even days, was done in minutes.

As she read through the AI's recommendations, she realized that the technology wasn't just saving her time—it was enhancing the quality of her research. The AI had found a precedent from a lesser-known case in a different jurisdiction that perfectly aligned with her client's situation. Meera smiled for the first time in days, knowing she had just turned the tide in her client's favor.

Indispensable AI Tools for Legal Research and Case Management

---

This chapter delves into how AI tools are transforming traditional legal research. It compares AI-driven legal research platforms with conventional methods, highlighting their advantages and applications.

Legal research and case management are at the heart of any legal practice. These activities are undoubtedly time-consuming, yet very prone to human error. This traditionally consists of long, arduous hours that lawyers put in poring over case law, statutes, and legal opinion to frame arguments, besides balancing administration e.g., the tedium of management of case files, tracking deadlines, and compliance with rules of procedure. The process is exhaustive, but not without its bottlenecks.

Now, enter Generative AI, an innovation promising to drive these tasks down the conveyor belt of efficiency and enable legal people to do what they truly excel in: the dispensation of justice.

- **The Pre-AI Era**: Traditional Legal Research and Case Management To appreciate just how incredibly transformative the introduction of Generative AI has been, there is merit in briefly referring back to a discussion about the traditional approaches to the practice of legal research and case management.

- **Legal Research**: Traditionally, the process of legal research has been immensely manual. This would require lawyers and paralegals to spend hours, if not days, researching in the law libraries, looking through physical copies of case reporters, statutes, and legal commentaries for precedents and relevant statutes or legal principles. Of course, things partly improved when digital databases entered the scene, yet this was still highly resource- and time-intensive work. There was always that risk of having one crucial piece of information pass by unnoticed amidst the sea of information.

- **Case Management**: In regard to case management, the traditional mechanism of keeping records in physical files and tracking the deadlines manually to ensure that documents were filed timely and correctly-the administrative burden was pretty heavy, and any single lapse amounted to a serious blow to the case. Further, the lack of centralized systems ensured inefficiencies in several instances, with different team members working from different versions of documents or missing out on key updates. These processes, though comprehensive, were anything but efficient. They required a serious investment of time and resources, time much better spent on other, more strategic areas of legal practice.

The Bottlenecks in Traditional Approaches

Traditionally, there have been a number of bottlenecks in the areas of legal research and case management:

1. **Time-Consuming Research**: In the traditional or conservative sense, research then involves weeding through an insurmountable pile of information by the lawyers themselves, a laborious process in which human error can easily occur. The bulk and the ever-growing nature of case law, statute books, and volumes of legal writing mean that even the most conscientious researcher may overlook an important precedent or legal principle.

2. **Disorganized Case Management**: With no central automated system, the case management process becomes manual and prone to errors. Deadlines can be missed, files misplaced, and communication with team members disjointed-resulting in delays and even threats to the procedural outcome of a case.

3. **Resource-Intensive Processes**: Legal research and case management are resource-intensive procedures, requiring immense investment in human capital. For small firms or solo practitioners, this could be really crippling, while larger law firms may find it too consuming, limiting the number of new matters they can accept due to the possible scarcity of personnel and time to devote to such matters.

    o **The Emergence of Generative AI**: A New Direction in the Practice of Law Generative AI solves many of the problems inherent in traditional legal research and case management. Automation of routine tasks, faster and more accurate legal research, and smoothing case management processes are some of the things AI can greatly improve in legal practices.

- o **AI in Legal Research**: This was where AI-powered tools, such as ROSS Intelligence and LexisNexis, transformed the capability to conduct legal research using NLP supported by machine learning, thereby enabling the computer to understand complex queries in law and pull out relevant results quickly. These tools analyze huge case laws, statutes, and legal opinions and extract from them summaries and insights which a human researcher would take a long time, even days, to compile.

- o **Example:** ROSS Intelligence enables attorneys to ask legal questions in natural language and provide answers with specific case law and legal analytics. For instance, a question such as "What are the key precedents for breach of contract under Indian law?" may be asked and a detailed response obtained, summing up the relevant cases and thus saving hours of research time.

How AI Stands Out from Traditional Research Tools

A relevant and important question that many legal practitioners ask, especially those who are accustomed to traditional legal research tools like **SCC Online, CTC Online,** and **AIR Manual** - how is **AI-powered legal research** different from and improves upon these traditional platforms that are being used by many practioners of law:

1. **AI Provides Deeper Contextual Understanding**

   - o Traditional research platforms such as SCC Online and CTC Online primarily rely on **keyword searches**. Lawyers search for case law, statutes, or regulations by entering specific legal terms or phrases. This often leads to a **long list of results**, and the user must sift through the cases to find the most relevant ones.

   - o **AI-powered tools**, on the other hand, use **natural language processing (NLP)**, which allows lawyers to phrase their queries in plain language. For example, they can ask, *"What is the duty of care for a doctor in medical negligence cases?"* and the AI will return the most relevant cases without needing exact keywords.

- o AI goes beyond exact matches, offering **contextually relevant cases** even if the same words aren't used. This saves time and ensures more **thorough legal research** by retrieving conceptually similar cases, which may be missed through keyword-based searches.

- o **Reference: ROSS Intelligence**, for example, uses NLP to understand the legal question in a query, making research more intuitive and targeted than traditional methods like SCC Online.

2. **Predictive Case Outcomes**

- o AI doesn't just find relevant case law; it can also analyze historical rulings and **predict potential outcomes** based on patterns found in previous decisions.

- o For instance, in legal disputes, AI systems can evaluate **judge tendencies** and case patterns, offering insights on whether a judge tends to rule more favorably in similar cases. This predictive aspect is not available in traditional research tools.

- o **Example:** Tools like **Lex Machina** provide predictive analytics based on judge rulings, case trends, and more, giving lawyers a strategic advantage when planning litigation.

3. **Faster Legal Research and Document Review**

- o AI can **speed up legal research** significantly. What might take hours or even days using SCC Online or AIR Manual could be completed in a fraction of the time with AI.

- o AI tools can process **large volumes of documents** quickly and accurately, finding the most relevant parts of a case or law instantly. This improves the efficiency of tasks such as document discovery and contract analysis.

- o **Example: Kira Systems** for document analysis and **CaseText's CARA AI** for legal research are prime examples of how AI can cut down research time dramatically.

4. Customized Legal Insights

- AI tools can provide **customized insights** tailored to the specific needs of a case. They don't just return a list of cases but can provide **recommendations, strategies,** and even **relevant statutes** that apply to a particular situation.

- Traditional platforms offer access to large legal databases but don't analyze or organize the information specifically for the user's legal argument. AI platforms, on the other hand, can suggest **legal strategies** based on a combination of case law, statutes, and the specific details of a lawyer's query.

- **Example: ROSS Intelligence** provides custom insights based on the specifics of a query, guiding the lawyer to the best possible resources and arguments.

5. Continuous Learning and Updates

- AI platforms **learn and improve** over time. As more legal data is processed, these systems become better at understanding legal language, case patterns, and even **jurisdictional differences**.

- While SCC Online, CTC Online, and AIR Manual update their case law libraries regularly, they don't have the ability to **learn from user interactions** or improve their ability to provide better results over time.

- **Example:** AI platforms like **CaseText** use machine learning to continuously improve search accuracy and legal insights.

Addressing Common Concerns

- **"Can AI replace traditional research tools?"**

AI isn't meant to replace SCC Online, AIR Manual, or similar platforms. Instead, it enhances and complements traditional tools by providing **deeper insights, faster results,** and **contextual understanding** that go beyond keyword-based searches. Many lawyers may still prefer to use both in tandem—AI for deeper analysis and traditional platforms for specific queries or case law citations.

- **"Will AI compromise the thoroughness of research?"**

AI-powered platforms often enhance research thoroughness by finding cases or legal principles that a traditional tool might miss due to its reliance on exact keyword matching. With AI, legal professionals can feel more confident that they've uncovered all relevant case law and statutes for their arguments.

- **AI in Case Management**: Tools like Clio and CaseMine inducted AI right into the mainstream of case management by automating tasks such as tracking deadlines, managing documents, and communicating with clients. These platforms offer a centralized system wherein all case-related information is stored, ensuring that team members are always working with the most current information.

  - **Example:** Clio is a cloud-based case management system using AI for automating routine jobs, such as scheduling, billing, and document management. It comes with special features to automatically track deadlines and send reminders so that no critical date will ever be missed. Furthermore, AI-driven analytics powered by Clio can provide insight into the status of any case to aid lawyers in making informed decisions.

The Impact of Generative AI on Judges: Pre- versus Post-Scenario

Judges, too, in the same way as lawyers, stand to benefit tremendously in cases that involve legal research and case management when Generative AI is used. Let me explain this using an example involving a judge who presided over a complex civil litigation case:

- **No AI Era:** A high court judge has to give judgment in a complex civil litigation case with several parties and complicated points of law. The case demands that the judge goes through a lot of evidence, legal briefs, and precedents. This means the judge, with the small clerical staff, needs to go through hundreds of pages manually to identify relevant case law and ensure that all the requirements for procedures are adhered to. This is cumbersome and predisposes him to overlook important information. The complex issues, together with the volume of materials, which were being contributed to, caused a delay in the time needed to deliver judgment, hence the tardy delivery of timely justice.

- **Post-AI scenario**: Years later, that same judge has the use of Generative AI-powered tools for doing legal research and case management. The judge can refer to an AI-powered research tool like ROSS Intelligence, which quickly identifies applicable relevant precedents and, with a deep understanding, provides a comprehensive summary of the statements of key legal principles related to the case. The AI system cross-references the case law against the facts of the current case, bringing up any potential discrepancies or areas of the case that require extra attention.

  From the perspective of case management, a CaseMine-like AI-powered system would assist the judge in monitoring dates that have expired or will expire, manage the records in chronological order, and thereby meet all the formal requirements. It also gives real-time updates and reminders, reducing the administrative work for the judge and his assistants. The judge, therefore, is free to give his time to analyzing the legal arguments proffered, reviewing the evidence led, and writing a well-reasoned judgment.

- **The Result**: The decisions come sooner and with greater veracity due to the advent of AI. The judge is well-placed to make a timely determination believing that all legal principles and precedents have been considered, let alone those relevant. Applying AI to case management implies that no steps in the procedure can be overlooked, thus limiting the appeals based on technical grounds or administrative oversights.

Overcoming the AI Adoption Humps

While advantages of Generative AI in legal research and case management are obvious, this acceptance of technology does not come without its set of challenges. The judicial fraternity of both judges and lawyers will feel some kind of aversion for this newly introduced AI, as it may set them back or result in inaccuracies. These could be overcome by proper training and an understanding that AI is just a tool, enhancing human judgment, not replacing it entirely. Building trust in AI is the first and foremost thing that has to be done while implementing AI. Lawyers and other professionals should understand that it was designed to help and support, not to replace them.

In doing so, AI increases the quality of the work done by lawyers and frees time to be able to concentrate on more challenging, subtle areas of their practice. Another concern would be the accuracy of the results put forward by AI. AI tools are prone to making mistakes, great as they are. The legal professional should always check the content the AI generates for its accuracy and applicability. As time goes on, people will get used to using AI and learn how to utilize its powers more effectively. Smooth integration of AI into an existing workflow:

Finally, the challenge rests on how to integrate the AI tools with the existing workflow. Most AI platforms are designed in a user-friendly manner and can easily integrate into their existing case management system. Gradual adoption of AI, starting with simple and progressively increasing in difficulty, is considered to give a smooth transition to AI-driven practices for both law firms and courts.

Hands-on learning: experimenting with AI tools To get the most out of what generative AI has to offer for legal research and case management, I would encourage you to try working with some of the tools discussed in this chapter.

Using one of the AI legal research platforms, such as ROSS Intelligence, do research on a current case. Note how this tool identifies relevant case law and legal principles, and compare your results against your traditional ways of doing legal research. You will probably find that AI can make the time you put into research far less demanding, leaving you free to concentrate on the more strategic elements of the case.

Take a closer look at the example of an AI-driven case management system, such as Clio. Try managing a small case on the system-from keeping track of deadlines and managing documents to communicating with the client through it. Observe how such automation releases your time and lessens the administrative burden of your team.

For judges, try introducing an AI research tool into your workflow. Leverage the tool in cross-referencing case law and creating summaries, observing how this will further assist you in making well-informed and timely decisions. In this respect, substantial efficiency gains from AI afford you a greater degree of ease and confidence when handling complicated cases. By integrating these AI tools into your practice, you can also witness the magic of Generative AI at work in the legal world. The future of law is not just about using state-of-the-art technologies but leveraging such technologies.

Questions for Reflection

1. **Efficiency vs. Quality:**

   How does AI enhance the efficiency of legal research? Are there any trade-offs in terms of the quality or depth of research?

   ____

   ____

   ____

   ____

   ____

   ____

   ____

   In what ways can AI improve the accuracy and relevance of legal research findings?

   ____

   ____

   ____

   ____

   ____

   ____

2. **Data Management and Privacy:**

With AI handling vast amounts of legal data, what are the key privacy concerns that need to be addressed?

____

____

____

____

____

____

____

How can AI systems ensure that sensitive legal data is protected from breaches and misuse?

____

____

____

____

____

____

____

3. **AI's Role in Complex Cases:**

How might AI assist in complex legal cases that require deep analysis of precedents and statutes? Could it miss the nuances that a human researcher would catch?

____

____

____

____

____

____

____

What are the limitations of AI in understanding the context and implications of legal precedents?

____

____

____

____

____

____

____

Scenario for Debate

Consider a scenario where an AI tool provides legal research that conflicts with a lawyer's intuition and experience. The AI's findings are based on the latest case law, while the lawyer's approach is rooted in older, foundational cases.

- **Debate Topic**: Which should take precedence in court—the AI's data-driven research or the lawyer's experienced-based judgment? Discuss the roles of intuition and data in legal practice.

Hands-On Exercise

Use an AI-powered legal research tool (if available) to find precedents related to a specific legal issue. Compare the AI's findings with those you can find through traditional research methods. Reflect on the differences in speed, depth, and relevance.

CHAPTER FOUR: STRENGTHENING EFFICIENCY IN COURT OPERATIONS THROUGH AI

AI-ENHANCED CASE MANAGEMENT

Vignette: *The Tides of Justice*

In the bustling city of Chennai, Judge Aarthi had become accustomed to the endless stream of cases flowing through her courtroom. The caseload was overwhelming, with no signs of slowing down. The court's manual case management system was archaic, and it often felt like she was drowning in a sea of paperwork.

But today, she was introduced to something different—a new AI-powered case management system called "Causelist." The system was designed to streamline the scheduling of hearings, track case progress, and prioritize cases based on urgency and complexity.

Curious, Judge Aarthi logged into Causelist and was immediately struck by its simplicity and efficiency. The AI had already analyzed her docket, identifying cases that were likely to be resolved quickly and those that required more attention. It suggested optimal hearing schedules, taking into account the availability of witnesses, lawyers, and other involved parties.

For the first time in months, Judge Aarthi felt in control. The AI had not only helped her organize her docket but had also provided insights that she could use to manage her time more effectively. As she began her day, she noticed a change—a smoother flow, a more manageable pace. It was as if the tides of justice were finally turning in her favor.

Strengthening Efficiency in Court Operations through AI

Exploring the use of AI to enhance courtroom procedures, this chapter covers automation of administrative tasks, case management, real-time legal assistance, and evidence organization.

The Indian judiciary is multi-tiered, right from the local magistrate courts to the High Courts and the Supreme Court. The procedures of each such court are specific to the nature of, and complexity involved in, the litigation dealt with by it. Yet, there are common practices across all levels, including some procedural bottlenecks, like preparation and submission of evidence, hearing dates, and management of case documents-all areas where Generative AI can play a transformational role.

The current chapter will look at how AI can smooth out some of the common courtroom procedures that take place in courts of law and will also be beneficial for the concerned lawyers and judges. We look at pre-trial work that lawyers can do using AI and also some ideas about how judges could make use of AI during and after courtroom arguments are presented.

A look at the age without AI in perspective:

Common Courtroom Procedures Before appreciating the impact of AI, we first consider the traditional procedures followed in courts of law in India.

1. **Preparation and Submission of Evidence**: Lawyers normally invest extensive time in preparing, marshaling, and presenting evidence. This includes drafting supporting affidavits, compiling documents, and ensuring that all evidence is procedurally admissible. In complicated cases, this may require the tedious examination of several thousand pages of documents-a process that is not only time-consuming but also prone to human error.

2. **Scheduling Hearings**: There is also scheduling of hearings, which poses a challenge to courts in those cases where there may be multiple parties involved or cases that require a large number of witnesses. Delays happen because hearings are postponed or rescheduled due to conflicts from the manual coordination of schedules.

3. **Case Document Management**: Most of the case records, in most jurisdictions, even in the lower courts, are maintained and managed manually. This involves everything from the actual keeping of

documents to monitoring case developments and updating of records. Such lack of digitization and automation can easily result in lost or misplaced files that only continue to delay case resolution.

4. **Courtroom Proceedings**: In-court proceedings rely on manual notes, physical documents, and verbal testimonies by the judge and lawyers. Lack of real-time analysis tools implies decisions are prima facie based on a judge's memory or manual cross-referencing of legal texts, which may be inefficient and lead to inconsistencies.

Emergence of Generative AI:

Changing Courtroom Processes Generative AI could make these courtroom procedures much faster, more accurate, and smooth. Let's now see how AI can be used in every stage of the courtroom process. AI in preparation and submission of evidence: Lawyers can then use AI to automate the preparation and lodging of that evidence. AI tools, such as Luminance and eBreviacan, can consider a very large volume of documents for relevant information and even begin to draft summaries or affidavits from information derived from that data. This not only accelerates the process but also diminishes the possible introduction of mistakes.

Example: In a complex commercial litigation matter, a lawyer might utilize Luminance to review several thousand contract documents in a fraction of the time that such a task would take to review manually. The AI identifies important clauses, flags potential issues, and provides a summary report upon which the lawyer can rely in preparing for trial. This frees the lawyer to strategy rather than getting bogged down in document review.

- **AI in Scheduling of Hearings**: AI also helps in scheduling hearings. Among other tools, LegalSifter and CourtSage leverage the power of AI to digest case data and provide optimal dates when hearings are most likely to be scheduled based on party availability, case complexity, and court calendar. This can significantly reduce delays due to scheduling conflicts.

- o **Example:** A High Court judge can trust CourtSage to automatically schedule hearings in a multi-party civil case. The AI would take into consideration the availability of all parties, based on the estimated time for each hearing, before developing a schedule that best minimizes delays and avoids conflicts. This will help the case to move as smoothly as possible through the court system.

- **AI in the Management of Case Documents**: Another area where AI can really make a difference is document management. Using case management software powered by AI, such as CaseMine and Clio, automatically updates the case files on time, monitors case development, and ensures the documents are readily available. This minimizes the chances of lost or misplaced files and ensures judges and lawyers always have the most updated information at their fingertips.

  - o **Example:** There are hundreds of running cases in a busy District Court that CaseMine could handle by digitizing the case files. The AI automatically categorizes documents, changes, and edits while keeping updates on case statuses in real time. That ensures the latest status of any case is available to all parties involved, avoiding unnecessary administrative delays and improving the overall efficiency of the court.

- **AI for In-Court Proceedings**: AI can present data analysis in real time, suggest relevant case law, and even provide testimony transcription support during in-court proceedings. Tools such as ROSS Intelligence and LexisNexis integrate into the courtroom to allow judges to access pertinent legal information immediately and cross-reference case law at will.

  - o **Example:** Suppose a judge has been assigned to preside over a complex criminal trial. In that process, the judge has to reach for a references bundle with previous case law in view to determine whether some evidence would be admissible. ROSS Intelligence installed in this courtroom enables the judge to key in a query and immediately obtain a summary of case law relevant to your query with an analysis of how those cases apply to your case. This not only speeds up the process of decision-making, but also the rulings are given based on the most apt and current information.

- **Scenarios Pre- and Post-AI**: A Critical Comparison here is a practical situation that helps to understand how AI would impact and alter courtroom procedures, from a lawyer's and a judge's perspective.

- **Pre-AI Scenario**: An attorney gets ready for a High Court case of high-profile corporate fraud. This will involve the study of thousands of financial documents, emails, and contracts in hope of finding something to pin on the case. The process is painfully slow since all the documents have to be manually gone through by the lawyer himself. This means he needs to spend weeks studying documents. Meanwhile, the case gets delayed because the court is not able to coordinate schedules among various parties concerned lawyer.

- **Post-AI Scenario**: Now the same lawyer uses Luminance for document review. AI identifies patterns of fraud, underlines the relevant sections of that document, and even drafts a preliminary report. This allows the lawyer to review the documents in a matter of days instead of weeks. The court in turn uses CourtSage for scheduling. This solution rapidly finds dates that all parties are mutually available, continuing the case with no unnecessary delays.

- **Pre-AI Scenario (Judge)**: A case of disputes over multiple properties comes before the judge presiding over the lower court. First, he has to go through each party's submissions and compare those with precedents in law because each and every procedural requirement has to be observed. It is slow and full of delays since he needs time to get the documents delivered and filed physically.

- **Post-AI Scenario-Judge**: Case management on CaseMine by the judge, ROSS Intelligence during arguments in court: CaseMine digitizes all filings and organises them issue-wise, along with keeping a tab on deadlines of each. During the trial, ROSS Intelligence on the bench presents before the judge the latest case law on any proposition of law thrown up thus enabling him to pronounce his decision. The AI transcribes the proceedings so the judge can pay more attention to the arguments rather than note-taking.

- **The Results**: AI makes the work of a lawyer and a judge more effective. Free of administrative burdens, the lawyer will focus his efforts on building a good case, while the judge issues timely and better-informed decisions. The speed and accuracy of the judicial process increase in general, to the benefit not only of the legal professionals but also of the clients and the public who depend on timely justice being served.

Overcoming the Challenges of AI Adoption While gains from Generative AI in streamlining courtroom procedures are evident, its adoption has not come without challenges. Legal professionals and judges alike may be concerned about the veracity of such AI tools, potential bias therein, and what it could mean for their independence in decision-making. However, careful implementation and continuous training will assuage these challenges.

- **Confidence in AI**: The judges and lawyers should regard the AI as augmenting their capabilities, not substituting them. If the courts start deploying AI on less critical tasks first, then build from it into more complex processes, the confidence in the technology will grow.

- **Bias and Fairness**: AI systems must be transparent and not discriminate in their practice. The courts should, therefore, favor those AI systems that allow explainability in their output and provide human intervention where necessary. Regular auditing and updating of the AI systems will go a long way in ensuring that these are nondiscriminatory and dependable.

- **Integration into Existing Workflows**: The incorporation of AI in the existing legal framework should be very well-thought-out. Courts can begin utilizing AI for administrative issues and then, over time, transition it into more depth-related substantive issues like case research and analysis. This will allow a natural evolution where legal professionals learn about the latest technology in an uncomplicated manner.

Experiential Training: Playing with AI Tools

I encourage you to implement some of the tools discussed in this chapter so that you can actually experience for yourself some of the benefits of Generative AI in court procedures. Look to use an AI-based scheduling tool like CourtSage and understand how that tool can ease up the court's hearing schedule. Observe how it fills up the courts' calendar, thus reducing waiting times as schedules had less conflict. Then try handling a small case with the help of any artificial intelligence-driven case management system like CaseMine. Keep track of the deadlines, documents, and see to it that all the formal requirements are met. This would free your time and lessen the administrative burden on your team since much of the routine tasks have been automated.

For judges, try working into your workflow something like ROSS Intelligence, an AI research tool. During the proceedings, use it to make case law and legal analysis available in real time. You'll find AI enhancements a great way to make better-informed, real-time decisions. Integrated into your courtroom practices, you will no doubt start to see the transformative power of generative AI.

The future of the judiciary is not just about adopting new technologies; using those technologies in the best possible way to achieve better and more equitably delivered justice and making sure the system serves everyone promptly and effectively.

Questions for Reflection

1. **Efficiency Gains:**

   How does AI enhance the efficiency of case management in the judiciary? What are the key areas where AI can have the most significant impact?

   ____

   ____

   ____

   ____

   ____

   ____

   ____

   What challenges might arise in integrating AI with existing case management systems?

   ____

   ____

   ____

   ____

   ____

   ____

   ____

2. **Prioritization and Fairness:**

How can AI assist in prioritizing cases based on urgency and complexity? What are the potential risks of AI influencing the scheduling and flow of cases?

____

____

____

____

____

____

____

How can AI ensure that case management decisions are fair and unbiased?

____

____

____

____

____

____

____

3. **Human Oversight**:

What role should human oversight play in AI-enhanced case management? How can humans and AI collaborate effectively in managing cases?

In what scenarios might human intervention be necessary to correct or override AI recommendations?

Scenario for Debate

Imagine a scenario where AI suggests prioritizing certain cases based on algorithmic criteria, but a judge disagrees based on their knowledge of the cases' context and impact.

- **Debate Topic**: Should the judge override the AI's recommendations, or should the AI's data-driven approach take precedence? Discuss the balance between data and human judgment in case management.

Hands-On Exercise

Research and review an AI-powered case management system used in a legal setting. Evaluate its features, strengths, and weaknesses. Reflect on how it could be improved or adapted for different legal environments.

CHAPTER FIVE: GENERATIVE AI
FOR DRAFTING LEGAL DOCUMENTS
THE FUTURE OF LEGAL DRAFTING WITH AI

Vignette: The Final Draft

Maya, a senior legal consultant in Bengaluru, had seen it all when it came to drafting legal documents. She knew the art of crafting precise, watertight agreements, but she also knew the grind it took to get there—hours of drafting, reviewing, and redrafting. Today, however, was different.

The client, a fast-growing tech startup, needed a complex multi-jurisdictional contract drafted quickly. The stakes were high, and the timeline was tight. Maya decided to rely on a tool she had recently started experimenting with—an AI-driven drafting assistant called "DocuSmart."

As she entered the key terms and clauses, DocuSmart began generating the draft in real-time. It flagged potential issues, suggested clauses that were compliant with laws across multiple jurisdictions, and even cross-referenced with recent cases where similar contracts had faced legal challenges. The AI wasn't just drafting a document; it was crafting a strategy.

Maya reviewed the draft with a critical eye, making adjustments here and there, but for the most part, it was solid. In record time, she had a final draft ready for the client—one that she knew was not only legally sound but strategically robust.

As she sent the document off, Maya couldn't help but reflect on how far legal drafting had come. The hours she once spent poring over each detail were now freed up for higher-level thinking and client engagement. DocuSmart had transformed her role from a drafter of documents to a true legal strategist.

Generative AI for Drafting Legal Documents

A guide on how AI can be used to draft contracts, pleadings, and other legal documents. This chapter demonstrates how AI reduces manual errors, accelerates drafting time, and improves accuracy.

One of the most important tasks in the legal profession involves the drafting of legal documents. Indeed, whether one is preparing contracts, agreements, or pleadings, a great level of precision, legal acumen, and attention to detail is required. Traditionally, the process of legal document drafting has been tedious and requires a very considered usage of language, legal principles, and factual nuances. However, that is no longer the case with the emergence of Generative AI, as lawyers are now provided with some useful tools to make the process faster in drafting, with accuracy and compliance with the required standards in the legal field. This chapter discusses the capability of Generative AI to draft legal documents, including but not limited to contracts, agreements, pleadings, and briefs. We shall describe here a step-by-step methodology for the preparation, review, and validation of key points against these documents using AI and point out how AI changes this fundamental aspect of the work of a lawyer.

The Pre-AI Era: Traditional Document Drafting Under the traditional and conservative legal environment, drafting legal documents involved the following:

1. **Understanding Client Needs**: The first step in the preparation of any legal document requires understanding the client's objectives and legal needs. This is achieved by meeting with clients, reviewing supporting documents, and compiling relevant facts.

2. **Legal Research**: After recording the needs of the client, a draft of the legal document has to be prepared based on the necessary research into laws, regulations, and case precedents to ensure that it is legally perfect so that full protection can be extended to the client.

3. **Document Creation**: Next, the lawyer creates the document, taking a pre-defined format or boilerplate text as a starting point. This is very time-consuming because it requires fitting the document to what the client precisely needs to say and yet render it clear, precise, and legally correct.

4. **Review and Revision**: When the first draft is complete, the document undergoes numerous cycles of review and revision. This may involve collaboration with other lawyers, the integration of client comments, and fine-tuning of wording.

5. **Validation**: The last step involves validation that the document is legally valid and binding. The activities to be done include verification that the document complies with prevailing laws, that all parties who need to sign have signed the document, and that the terms of the document are enforceable. The traditional approach is comprehensive but error-prone, delayed, and inconsistent.

We shall see how each of these steps could be different with Generative AI.

Generative AI: The Magic in Document Drafting

Generative AI technology can save loads of time and effort in drafting legal documents. With the help of NLP supported by machine learning, AI will be able to automate most of the documentation processes while improving their accuracy and uniformity.

Here's how AI can help with different types of documents:

- **Contracts**: This would probably be one of the most common legal documents. They come in many forms, like employment, leasing, sale of goods, and many more. Generative AI is used in multiple applications to help lawyers create contract templates, identify important clauses to review, and suggest language given the specific details of a transaction using applications such as LegalMation and DocuSign CLM.

- **Pleadings and Briefs**: These, in a case or litigation, are some of the most prominent documents where the legal arguments and positions of parties are elaborated upon. AI-powered systems, such as ROSS Intelligence and Casetext, assist attorneys in preparing pleadings through an analysis of legal precedents and suggesting arguments from previous cases.

- **Agreements**: Non-disclosure agreements can be prepared using artificial intelligence tools, for example Luminance, which scan key provisions and raise flags on inconsistencies or omitted clauses among others on partnership and business agreements.

Breaking It Down Step by Step in AI Use in the Creation of Legal Documents

Let's now proceed to break down the process of drafting legal documents into step-by-step actions with the incorporation of artificial intelligence at every step of the way:

1. **Understanding the Client's Needs**: The human touch is irreplaceable, even with AI, forms the backbone of document creation in the initial stages. This involves the communication between lawyers and their clients to understand the goals, issues, and specific needs a client has for the document in question by way of interviewing the client and collecting supportive documentation. The work could also be aided by AI, which can sort and categorize the information available about the client and underline the most essential details for the draft. Tools like Luminance will be able to read the client documents automatically and extract and categorize relevant data to speed up the process of gathering essential information.

2. **Researching Legal Requirements:** Ordinarily, lawyers would need to take several hours and even days to research the legal precedents, statutes, and regulations applicable to the case or transaction at hand. AI can greatly reduce this time by providing instant access to relevant case law and legal rules. AI-powered tools include ROSS Intelligence and Casemine, which help attorneys locate relevant legal authorities more quickly, summarize case law, and even sometimes suggest possible legal arguments. AI systems sort out oceans of legal data, extracting from it relevant statutes and judicial opinions to guide the creation process.

   o **Example:** If you're writing a contract on intellectual property rights, ROSS Intelligence will have summaries of the latest court cases involving that type of contract in front of you in a flash, so your paper will remain current legally. Based on

3. **Writing the Paper**: This is really where Generative AI is phenomenal. Once the attorney has obtained all the information required and has researched what the law requires, then AI can take over with the actual creation of the document. LegalMation and DocuSign CLM are AI-driven platforms that have pre-designed templates which the lawyers can use and develop given the specifics of the case or transaction.

- o **Machine Learning**: the platforms apply algorithms to analyze the particular needs of the client and make suggestions regarding the languages of the contract. AI can auto-populate certain clauses with regard to the type of document being drafted.

- o **Example:** LegalMation can auto-draft key clauses on warranties, indemnities, and payment terms of a sales agreement based on whether the sale involves goods or services. It also identifies any risks and suggests mitigating language for those risks.

4. **Document Review**: Once the first draft is generated, there is the need to review such document for completeness, accuracy, and legal sufficiency. This often involves manual checks, but AI can help find mistakes, inconsistencies, and other potential risks.

   - o **AI Assistance:** Tools like Luminance and eBrevia apply natural language processing against legal documents to flag potentially disturbing language, missing clauses, or other legal pitfalls. It can also ensure that the document is within the ambit of applicable laws and regulations.

   - o **Example:** Suppose you are drafting a non-disclosure agreement. Luminance can point out missed confidentiality clauses and propose the right language to guard both parties concerned in said agreement.

5. **Validating Key Points:** The last step is verification of the key provisions within the document to ensure they will remain legally binding and enforceable. This includes confirmation that the parties have signed the document, it contains clauses necessary for the legal stipulations, and the whole setup according to the standard legal requirements.

   - o **AI Assistance:** AI can also cross-check the document for missing information with other similar documents; thus, you can be sure no clause that is supposed to appear in the document is left out. Tools such as DocuSign CLM also provide digital signatures, which will make your document legally binding.

   - o **Example:** In case you are developing an employment contract, AI would make sure all the required clauses about compensation, notice of termination, or even non-compete agreements have been included under prevailing labor laws and are binding.

Types of Legal Documents and AI's Role in Drafting

Let's take a close look at how Generative AI can help with various types of legal documents:

1. **Employment Contracts** Employment contracts tend to be lengthy, often with elaborate sections on compensation, benefits, termination, and no-compete provisions. Using an AI-based tool such as LawGeex, employment contract templates could be generated with automatic customization based on specific terms agreed upon between employer and employee.

   ○ **Example:** LawGeex can draft an employment agreement on performance bonuses, stock option agreements, and non-disclosure agreements. It flags unclear terms and provisions that are invalid or missing automatically.

2. **Partnership Agreements** These are the agreements that describe the role, responsibility, and profit-sharing agreement between business partners. The documents may be complicated, especially when there are several parties concerned. AI systems like Luminance support the creation of partnership agreements by evaluating other agreements and then recommend provisions that may come closer to business norms.

   ○ **Example:** If you are drafting a partnership agreement for a tech startup, Luminance may suggest sections on intellectual property ownership, decision-making processes, and profit-sharing arrangements while highlighting areas where potential conflicts of interest may arise and offering mitigating language.

3. Non-Disclosure Agreement NDAs are usually used to protect confidential information in business transactions. Examples of AI tools, like eBrevia, can then automatically generate an NDA by identifying key provisions relating to the confidentiality undertaking, duration of the agreement, and scope of disclosure.

   ○ **Example:** eBrevia can automatically draft an NDA for a client who is engaging in negotiations with a potential investor. The AI ensures the agreement provides protection for proprietary information, protection of trade secrets, and protection of financial data. The flag for clauses that may expose the client to unnecessary risk is also raised.

4. **Sales of goods contracts** outline the terms of any transaction between a buyer and a seller, including but not limited to payment terms, delivery schedules, and warranties. AI tools, like LegalMation, can generate these contracts based on the analysis of the specific transaction and make suggestions as to appropriate language.

   o **Example:** LegalMation can draft a sales contract between a manufacturer of goods and a retailer. The AI prepares sections on payment terms, delivery schedules, and warranties, ensuring that the contract will protect both parties and also help in following all related trade laws.

   o **Pre- and Post-AI Scenario**: A Comparative Analysis To help put that into perspective, to understand the transformational power of AI in drafting legal documents, consider a comparative scenario where a law firm is called upon to draft a complex merger agreement.

   o **Scenario Pre-AI**: The mandate to draft a merger agreement between two large corporations lands with a medium-sized law firm. It involves countless rounds of client meetings to understand the merger terms, extensive research of the lawbook to ensure the transaction conforms strictly to corporate laws, and a laborious manual drafting of various clauses that would cover every eventuality. The first draft goes into literally dozens of revisions before different teams within the firm review the language, suggest changes, and ensure that all legal and financial aspects are brought out or represented. This easily takes a few weeks to accomplish, and this is quite labor-intensive and hence costly.

   o **Scenario after AI**: Today, the same law firm employs Generative AI applications such as Luminance and LegalMation to draft the merger agreement. After having several client meetings to collect the needed information, attorneys input key terms and conditions into the AI system.

The AI therefore drafts an agreement, automatically including relevant clauses from previous similar transactions and the latest legal requirements. It highlights the potential risks, shows alternative language, and points to missing clauses. What previously took weeks from drafting to final review now can be done in days.

- **The Output**: AI saves much time and effort in drafting the merger agreement. For the law firm, it can release them to invest more resources in taking on additional clients or diving deeper into further complex legal strategy development. The final document will be wholesomely accurate, complete, and customized according to the needs of the client, in full compliance with all the relevant laws, with minimal risk.

- **Conclusion**: The Future of Legal Document Drafting with AI This is a chapter that covers nearly all aspects of how this generative AI will turn upside down the conventional way of legal document drafting. As this AI automates much of the routine work, improves accuracy, and offers data-driven insights, it allows lawyers to create superior-quality legal documents in a fraction of the time taken conventionally.

Artificial Intelligence applied in the drafting of contracts, pleadings, and agreements does not have to relate merely to issues of efficiency but also in enhancing the practice of law. It would now be possible for lawyers to devote themselves to the more creative and strategic components of their work, knowing full well that the foundational elements of the documents being prepared will be handled with precision and care by AI.

As these AI tools become more integrated into your practice, remember that the goal is not to take away from the human element but to add to it. The best and most successful legal practices will be ones using AI in complement with their expertise to make sure every document produced is both legally sound and fits the goals of the clients.

The future of legal document drafting has arrived, and Artificial Intelligence powers it. By embracing these tools, you position yourself and your practice at the leading edge of innovation in the law to take on whatever the increasingly complex legal landscape throws your way.

Questions for Reflection

1. **The Role of AI in Legal Strategy:**

How might AI influence legal strategy through drafting? Can AI-generated documents anticipate and counter legal challenges effectively?

____

____

____

____

____

____

What are the limitations of AI in understanding the strategic nuances of legal drafting?

____

____

____

____

____

____

2. **Adaptability and Flexibility:**

How adaptable are AI-driven drafting tools to different legal systems and jurisdictions? Can they account for cultural and legal variations across borders?

____

____

____

____

____

____

____

In what ways can AI tools be customized to fit the specific needs of different law practices?

____

____

____

____

____

____

____

3. **Ethical Considerations in AI Drafting:**

What ethical concerns arise when AI is used to draft legal documents that have significant impacts on people's lives or businesses?

____

____

____

____

____

____

____

How should responsibility be assigned when an AI-generated document leads to legal complications or disputes?

____

____

____

____

____

____

____

Scenario for Debate

Consider a scenario where an AI tool drafts a complex international contract. After it's finalized, a discrepancy is found that could have significant legal repercussions.

- **Debate Topic**: Should the law firm take responsibility for the AI's error, or should the blame be shared with the AI developers? Discuss the ethical implications of AI-generated legal documents.

Hands-On Exercise

Draft a legal document that involves multiple jurisdictions using both traditional and AI-powered methods. Compare how each method handles the complexity of legal requirements across borders. Reflect on the advantages and limitations of AI in this context.

CHAPTER 6: AI-ENHANCED DECISION SUPPORT FOR JUDGES

Vignette: The Trial of Justice

The courtroom was silent, the kind of silence that presses in on you, making every shuffle and cough echo like a thunderclap. Judge Mehra, a seasoned judge with over three decades of experience, sat behind the bench, her expression stern but contemplative. Before her stood the defendant, a middle-aged man accused of embezzling millions from his employer—a case that had captured the media's attention and polarized public opinion.

As the prosecutor delivered his closing arguments, Judge Mehra's mind wandered to the piles of evidence she had reviewed over the past few weeks. Financial statements, emails, witness testimonies—all meticulously documented but overwhelming in volume. The complexities of modern financial crimes were not what they used to be when she first donned the robes.

A soft chime on her tablet snapped her back to the present. It was the AI assistant, a tool recently introduced into the court's operations. Dubbed "Nyaya," meaning justice, the AI was designed to analyze the evidence, cross-reference it with similar cases, and provide judges with a data-supported summary of possible outcomes based on precedent.

Judge Mehra hesitated, her finger hovering over the screen. She had been skeptical of Nyaya at first, wary of relying on a machine to guide her decisions. After all, what could a computer know about the nuances of human intent, the gray areas of morality, the weight of justice? But the case in front of her was a labyrinth of numbers and deceit, and time was of the essence.

With a decisive tap, she opened the AI's report. Instantly, a visual representation of the case's key elements appeared: a timeline of events, a summary of financial transactions, and, most intriguingly, a list of similar cases from the past decade, complete with their outcomes. The AI highlighted patterns she had not immediately noticed—small discrepancies in the testimonies, inconsistencies in the defendant's financial records that had eluded even the forensic accountants.

But it wasn't just the facts that Nyaya presented. The AI offered potential legal arguments, outlining how previous judges had interpreted similar evidence and what legal principles they had applied. It even suggested possible sentences, showing how they varied depending on the interpretation of the defendant's intent and the impact on the victims.

Judge Mehra took a deep breath, absorbing the information. The AI wasn't making the decision for her; it was offering a perspective, a way to sift through the noise and focus on what truly mattered. She could feel the weight of the decision, but for the first time in this case, it felt manageable.

The trial resumed, and as Judge Mehra delivered her judgment, she did so with the confidence that she had considered every angle, every possibility. Nyaya had not replaced her judgment; it had enhanced it, making her more certain that justice was being served.

Outside, as she stepped into the light of the setting sun, she thought about the future. She knew that AI would continue to evolve, becoming an ever-present partner in the quest for justice. And for the first time, she felt that the future of the judiciary was not just in safe hands—it was in wise ones.

AI-Enhanced Decision Support for Judges

Focusing on how AI can support judges, this chapter examines how data-driven insights from AI can assist in complex decision-making processes, enhancing objectivity and efficiency in rulings.

The heaviest load in the courtroom often falls to judges. From presiding over civil and company law to criminal cases, judges are called upon to sort out thorny legal issues, wade through volumes of evidence, and ensure that their findings of fact and decisions are legally correct but also fair. Matters worsen, or even become more stark, in the case of appellate courts where judges have to go through the verdicts of the lower courts to take a call on whether these should be upheld or overturned.

This chapter deals with how Generative AI might be a strong helper for the judges to give unbiased, data-supported decisions leading to landmark judgments.

Traditional Judicial Decision-Making

To understand how AI can change the way judges make decisions, some background is useful with respect to the traditional approach that judges take in rendering their decisions.

1. **Review of Evidence and Testimony:** The judges consider every piece of evidence presented before the court during trial and take great pains to sift through physical evidence, eye and ear witness testimonies, expert opinion, etc.

2. **Legal Research:** Judges conduct extensive legal research to identify the statutes, case law, and principles of law applying to the case before them. This helps to ensure that decisions made on cases are done on recognized legal doctrine.

3. **Weight of Facts and Legal Principles:** The judge has to weigh the facts of the case against relevant legal principles to reach a fair and just verdict. At this stage, a delicate balancing act between logic, reasoning from the perspective of law, and ethical considerations occurs.

4. **Writing the Judgment:** The last step involves writing the judgment where the judge describes the reasoning, principle of law involved, and the decision reached. This judgment needs to be well-argued, comprehensive, and eloquently written. While comprehensive, the steps involved are very time-consuming and may be prone to errors. Judges might make an error in recognizing applied precedents or misinterpret complex legal doctrines, rendering decisions inconsistent.

The Rise of AI: A New Era in the Judiciary Generative AI is set to change how judges consider decisions through data extrapolation, real-time legal research, and predictive analytics to assist judges in making more informed, objective, and consistent decisions. Let's see its application in different types of cases. Some of them are as follows:

1. Civil Cases - Civil cases most frequently appear when private parties disagree over matters such as contracts, property, and torts. What this means in reality is that civil litigation can be complicated because the interpretation of contracts, assessment of damages, and determination of liability in civil cases are usually very difficult to establish.

   o **AI in Civil Cases:** AI can support judges in civil cases by reading great volumes of contract language, identifying relevant legal precedents, and even going so far as to predict likely outcomes based on similar cases. **Example:** For breach of contract, the AI tools, like ROSS Intelligence, will analyze the terms within the contract and compare those terms to a variety of different contracts from other cases to propose possible rulings using established legal principles.

   The AI might further identify ambiguities in the contract language and recommend interpretations in concert with case law.

   o **Handling Appeals in Civil Cases**: An appeal, when made to the higher court, requires the judge to go through the judgment pronounced by the lower court to identify errors in the application of the law or in finding facts. AI can help in pointing out various discrepancies in the judgment by the lower court with respect to the precedents in order to give a more clear view to the appellate judge as to where the original judgment might have gone wrong. **Example:** On an appeal on a property dispute, the AI may discover how other jurisdictions have disposed of similar cases to assist the appellate judge in assessing whether the lower court's decision is consonant with general legal trends. The AI shall also highlight any missed precedents that may affect the appellate outcome.

2. **Company Law Disputes:** Company law cases usually involve complex legal and financial issues such as company mergers and acquisitions, shareholder disputes, and any other issues of compliance with regulatory requirements. Judges presiding over these cases have to sift through complicated corporate structures and financial transactions to reach decisions that are compatible with the principles of company law. AI in disputes of Company Law: AI can help judges in reviewing documents concerning corporate structure, agreements of shareholders, and filing made with the regulators. It could also provide insights into similar disputes resolved in the past to assist a judge in arriving at decisions consistent with the interpretation of corporate law. **Example:** In a case involving a shareholder dispute, with charges of mismanagement, application of AI tools, such as Luminance, could review the minutes of board meetings, financial statements, and shareholder agreements for possible breaches in fiduciary duty. The AI will also match the facts of this case with similar shareholder disputes and suggest potential outcomes based upon precedents.

   o **Handling Appeals in Company Law:** While the appellate courts revisit company law disputes, they need to identify correctly whether the lower court applied the principles of corporate law. AI can contribute by cross-referencing the lower court's judgment with case law from other jurisdictions to ensure that the appellate ruling is aligned both nationally and internationally with standards in corporate law.

   o **Example:** In an appeal to a dispute over the merger of a company, AI could emphasize cases from other jurisdictions that would be relevant to assist the appellate judge in making a determination of whether or not the merger was done appropriately under the corporation code. AI can also be used to present a comparative analytic review of the financial aspects of the merger to ensure that the ruling is not only legally sound but economically justifiable as well.

3. **Criminal Cases** Some criminal cases are, in fact, the most difficult decisions a judge makes, with serious crimes such as murder, assault, and fraud. Therefore, it is necessary that the judge knows to what extent to consider evidence or intent by the accused, as well as application of the appropriate criminal statutes in determining the guilt or innocence of a defendant.

   o **AI in Criminal Cases**: AI can assist judges to review evidence, evaluate probabilities of recidivism, and locate relevant case law. Certain types of artificial intelligence, including PredPol and Compas, are used experimentally in many jurisdictions for assessing criminal hotspots and risk of reoffending. This raises ethical considerations, which have to be handled with great care.

   o **Example:** In a case of fraud, AI will analyze financial documents, email, and other electronic evidence for fraud patterns. The AI then can provide recommendations on the range of sentences based on similar cases and hence assist the judge in rendering a consistent and appropriate sentence.

   o **Criminal Appeals:** The appellate judge needs to go over the lower court's findings in a criminal appeal to identify whether any legal errors occurred. AI can aid by deep analysis of the evidence presented, pointing out inconsistencies in witness testimonies, and matching with other appeals so that the appellate decision is consonant with accepted legal precedents.

   o **Example:** Appeal case of a murderer wherein AI can explore the forensic evidence and match these with other similar convictions that have been overturned because of new evidence or procedural error. The AI will also be able to examine alternative explanations of the crime, which will be very useful for the appellate judge in reaching a decision.

Key Considerations for Judges Using AI

While AI has enormous benefits in judicial decision-making, it also throws up some critical considerations for the judges to bear in mind:

1. **Objectivity vs. Bias:** AI systems are only as objective as the data that trains them. Judges should be aware of the biases these algorithms may host and make sure not to rely entirely on the insights thrown up by AI. The human element of judgment and ethical consideration should always remain at the center of a decision.

2. **Transparency:** Judges have to make sure AI mechanisms are transparent in their working logics. The logic behind AI recommendations should be clear and understandable so the judges themselves can critically assess the extent to which those conclusions drawn by AI are valid.

3. **Legal Precedents:** Whereas AI may, indeed, provide enlightening background on the precedents, it should be of critical importance that judges will cross-check what comes out from AI against established legal tenets. AI shall support and not replace the judge's very own legal acumen.

4. **Ethical Implications**: The use of AI tools, including Compas, has raised ethical debates around the issues of predictive policing and sentencing in criminal cases. Judges have to have critical reflection on the ethical consequences entailed by the use of AI while delivering judgments to ensure fairness and equity.

   o **Making Landmark Judgments** with AI It is said that generative AI may be able to help judges even with landmark judgments-these are cases that can bring about a new legal precedent or can go a long way in affecting society. With data-driven insights, AI will help the judges find out the wider ramifications of their verdicts so that their decisions are not only legally correct but socially responsible also.

   o **Example of Landmark Judgment**: A high-profile case concerning digital privacy rights. AI would sift through global trends in privacy law, compare the case to similar landmark rulings from other jurisdictions, and present the judge with an overview of what this potential decision might mean to society. The judge can thus craft a ruling which, in addition to answering the specific legal issues before him, sets a good precedent to guide future cases into the digital age.

- ○ **Conclusion**: The Role of AI in Judicial Decision-Making Throughout this chapter, we have explored multiple methods in which generative AI is an especially valuable resource to judges, enhancing the decision-making process across different types of cases. Be it from civil disputes to criminal trials, AI does have the potential to offer insights powered by data, streamline legal research, and ensure judgements are consistent with legal precedents. However, it is a decision to apply AI to the judiciary that needs to be made in a very careful manner. There must be a balance between the objectivity of AI and human judgment the judges exercise to make decisions on cases that are fair, transparent, and ethnically sound. This will, in turn, allow the judges to complement AI in the rendering of decisions that are not only legally robust but actually help in the evolution of the legal system itself.

The integration of AI into their fold holds the future of the judiciary, whereby judges will be able to handle the developing complexity of modern law and deliver timely and transformative justice. As the legal landscape changes with time, there is no doubt that AI will shape up the landmark judgments of tomorrow.

Questions for Reflection

As you consider the potential of AI in enhancing judicial decision-making, reflect on the following questions:

1. **Balancing Technology and Human Judgment:**

   How can we ensure that AI remains a tool to enhance, rather than replace, human judgment in the courtroom?

   ____

   ____

   ____

   ____

   ____

   ____

   ____

   In what ways can judges retain their autonomy while still leveraging AI's data-driven insights?

   ____

   ____

   ____

   ____

   ____

   ____

   ____

   ____

2. **Ethical Dilemmas:**

What ethical concerns might arise when using AI to assist in judicial decisions, particularly in cases involving severe penalties or personal liberties?

____

____

____

____

____

____

How can biases in AI systems be identified and mitigated to ensure fair outcomes?

____

____

____

____

____

____

3. **Consistency vs. Individualized Justice:**

AI can help bring consistency to judicial rulings by analyzing past cases and suggesting standardized outcomes. However, how can we balance this with the need for individualized justice that takes into account the unique circumstances of each case?

____

____

____

____

____

____

____

____

4. **Transparency and Accountability:**

How transparent should AI systems be in the courtroom? Should judges be required to disclose the extent to which AI influenced their decisions?

____

____

____

____

____

____

Who should be held accountable if an AI-generated recommendation leads to an unjust outcome?

____

____

____

____

____

____

____

5. **Future Considerations:**

As AI technology continues to evolve, what new roles might it play in the judiciary that we haven't yet considered?

____

____

____

____

____

____

____

How should the legal system prepare for the integration of even more advanced AI technologies in the future?

Scenario for Debate

Imagine a future scenario where an AI system is capable of delivering a complete judicial verdict based on data inputs, past precedents, and real-time analysis. In this world, the judge's role is primarily to oversee the AI's process and intervene only when necessary.

- **Debate Topic:** Should such a system be implemented? Discuss the potential benefits and risks of this scenario, considering factors such as efficiency, fairness, accountability, and the preservation of human judgment in the legal process.

Hands-On Exercise

If you have access to AI-based legal tools (like ROSS Intelligence or CaseText), try using them to analyze a hypothetical legal scenario. Compare the AI's recommendations with your own understanding of the case. Reflect on where the AI adds value and where it may fall short.

CHAPTER 7: AI AND PUBLIC ACCESS TO LEGAL SERVICES

Vignette: The Rural Advocate

In a remote village in Tamil Nadu, where the nearest courthouse was miles away and legal aid was a luxury few could afford, Rani was known as the "Rural Advocate." Though not formally trained as a lawyer, Rani had a deep understanding of local laws and a passion for helping her community navigate legal challenges.

Today, Rani was using something new—an AI-driven mobile app called "NyayaSathi," designed to provide basic legal guidance in local languages. A neighbor, struggling with a land dispute, approached her for help. Normally, this would require a trip to the distant town, days of waiting, and significant expenses. But with NyayaSathi, Rani could provide immediate assistance.

The AI app guided her through a series of questions, analyzing the land records, the dispute history, and relevant legal statutes. It then generated a simple, easy-to-understand summary of the legal options available, complete with a draft petition that could be filed with the local authorities.

For the first time, Rani felt empowered to offer more than just advice—she could now provide practical, actionable solutions. The AI didn't replace her; it enhanced her ability to serve her community. As she handed over the documents to her neighbor, she realized that NyayaSathi was more than just an app—it was a bridge between the people and the justice they deserved.

AI-Driven Public Access to Legal Services

This chapter discusses AI's role in improving access to justice for the general public, especially through online dispute resolution platforms, virtual legal assistants, and AI-driven public legal services.

Public access to justice is a democratically ingrained principle. A concept integral to any properly functioning democracy, the notion of citizens being accorded the facility to seek and obtain legal redress assumes heightened importance in a populous and pluralistic country like India. India's large, diverse population is marked by high socioeconomic inequality, raising specific challenges to equal access to legal services.

The urban elite may buy their way through the best possible legal representation, but most Indians, particularly those hailing from middle-class and low-income backgrounds, are at the mercy of fortune as they try to make their way through the system.

The present chapter deals with the role of AI-driven legal services to enhance public access to justice, ensuring that no citizen in the country is prevented, by economic conditions, from receiving the justice to which he or she is entitled.

Public Access - Intrinsic to Democracy

The Constitution of India grants every citizen a right to equality before the law and equal protection of the laws under Article 14, denoting the right of access to justice. But all these constitutional guarantees remain mere words if the people at large cannot, in fact, enforce their legal rights.

In a democratic form of Government, the administration of justice must be easily accessible and not confined to the privileged few. It is specially so in a country like India where a large section of the population lives in rural areas and a greater section are steeped in poverty and illiteracy. Public access to the legal system is not solely the concern of courts and practitioners, but equally important in ensuring that the citizenry can make sense of and navigate the legal system, receive sound legal advice, and resolve disputes competently, fairly, and efficiently. In the absence of adequate public access, the rule of law is subverted, and the system of laws becomes an instrument of oppression rather than a method of recourse.

Access to Justice: Challenges in the Middle Class and Lower Demographics The middle class and lower-income groups are indeed the largest demographics in India and therefore face significant challenges in access to justice.

These are:

1. **Legal Service Costs**: high legal costs, which put quality legal representation beyond the reach of most Indians. This often results in the person dropping the matter or using an underqualified or overburdened public defender.

2. **Geographical Barriers**: The large geography of India implies that a significant proportion of rural citizens live very far away from the nearest court or legal aid center. This distance, exacerbated by generally poor transportation infrastructure, has meant that access to legal services is quite difficult for such persons.

3. **Linguistic Gap**: This constitutes another barrier. While English and Hindi are in wide usage in courts, millions of Indians use regional languages and might not have much proficiency in the languages used in the judiciary. It is for this reason that not only going through the legal documents but even understanding them, communicating with the legal professionals, and thus full participation of such persons in the legal process becomes complicated.

4. **Legal Illiteracy:** A large part of the population in India lacks even basic legal literacy. They may not know what their rights are, or due processes and the available legal remedies; this places many at the mercy of exploitation and makes them unable to pursue their legal rights.

How AI Can Improve Public Access to Justice AI-driven legal services can help turn these challenges into an opportunity to make justice much more accessible to both the middle class and poor in India.

Here's how:

1. Access To Affordable Legal Advice Through AI Chatbots And Virtual Assistants: AI-powered legal chatbots can provide legal advice to the masses at an affordable cost. Their NLP allows them to understand and respond to legal queries in real time, helping guide them on issues as mundane as property disputes, consumer rights, and other family-related cases.

- o **Example:** A platform like DoNotPay, often termed the "robot lawyer," can be adapted for the Indian context. This might give advice in several languages about fighting traffic fines, dealing with small claims, or disputes between landlords and tenants. Such a platform will bring legal consultations way below their current cost, which is excessively high beyond the reach of poor people unable to pay the high costs of legal services.

2. Artificial Intelligence Powered Apps Offering Localized Legal Services AI-powered mobile applications can be designed for various legal needs across different regions in India. They can provide legal information, templates, and step-by-step guides in regional languages, allowing for better facilitation of the legal system among those using them.

   - o **Example:** An application powered with AI, meant for rural users in Tamil Nadu or West Bengal, will then provide legal consultations in Tamil or Bengali, respectively. It will help them understand their rights based on local laws and guide them through filing a complaint or even asking for legal aid. This could be of particular use in cases related to land disputes or access to any government scheme. 3. AI for Legal Document Preparation: Some of the barriers to accessing justice include the unreadability of legal documents.

   - o AI can assist in drafting legal documents, thus making the process of filing complaints, drafting agreements, or submitting petitions without necessarily having to go through the services of an expensive lawyer easier.

   - o **Example:** An AI-based platform may assist a user in navigating through the actual process of drafting his will or an affidavit. In simple, successive steps and asking them in the language of their choice, the artificial intelligence may prepare a legally permissible document based on his situation. This shall be particularly beneficial for people in rural areas where they cannot afford professional legal assistance.

4. **Language Translation and Simplification:** AI can bridge the language gap in the Indian legal system through real-time translation and summarization of documents, court proceedings, and other related materials. This would let a non-English or non-Hindi-speaking person have a better view of their rights in the case, hence fully participating in their legal matter.

   o **Example:** Artificially intelligent tools, such as Google Translate or Bhashini, can be integrated with legal platforms for real-time translation of legal documents into regional languages. Also, AI can simplify complicated legal terminologies of the documents so that these are more accessible to persons with low legal literacy.

5. ODR Platforms AI-powered ODR platforms involve a different approach from court proceedings for minor civil disputes and small claims. These platforms introduce the ability for disputants to reach a settlement online, with AI supporting the negotiation and mediation of discussions toward a fair settlement.

   o **Example:** An AI-driven ODR platform can help settle small claims arising out of issues like non-payment of wages or defective products without the physical presence of the parties in court. The AI would scrutinize the proof, consider the legal standing of the opposite parties, and decide upon a fair and legally plausible settlement. It would be of particular help where access to courts in far-flung areas is difficult.

6. **AI-powered Legal Aid Services:** Legal aid institutions in India are always jam-packed with the number of cases to be dealt with and a lesser number of lawyers to handle them. AI can help alleviate this burden by triaging cases, identifying those that can be resolved through automated processes, and providing preliminary legal advice to clients.

   o **Example:** An integrated AI system at the legal aid centers will filter cases that come to them and provide preliminary advice. This way, lawyers dealing with legal aid can give more time to cases complicated and needing human intervention, thus keeping the simpler ones for AI-driven procedures. How to operate

AI-driven legal services in India While the gains which can be derived from AI-driven legal services are significant, a diverse and geographically dispersed population like India poses many challenges.

To effectively implement AI-driven legal services, the following issues must be taken into account:

1. **Geographical Accessibility:** AI-driven legal services should be made available on mobile devices so that even rural and interior parts of India can access them. Given that the penetration of mobile phones is considered high in rural areas, as well, the creation of AI-driven legal apps that run on basic smartphones and are also capable of offline functioning would be important.

2. **Linguistic and Cultural Sensitivities:** AI-infused legal services need to be made appropriate for the linguistic and cultural diversities of India. That is, one has to develop the capacity of AI mechanisms to understand and respond in various regional languages and dialects. Secondly, designs should be done in a manner that cultural sensitivities are borne in mind so that the legal advice is appropriate and relevant in the context in which the user is placed.

3. **Digital Literacy and Training:** With mobile phones in wide use, there is wide variation in the level of digital literacy across India. Unless this aspect is addressed, particularly for the vulnerable sections of society, it would be a Herculean task to see AI-driven legal services put to effective use. This mismatch can be sorted out through legal awareness programs, community training, and liaison with local NGOs.

4. **Partnerships with Legal Professionals and Institutions:** To ensure believability and wide acceptance, AI-driven legal service development needs to be underpinned by partnerships among legal professionals and institutions. In this regard, collaborations with bar associations, law schools, and organizations offering legal aid will help in making the development of AI tools relevant and tap into the wealth of experience that leading legal professionals have amassed over the years.

5. **Ethics and Governance:** The use of AI in providing legal services must be steeped in strong ethical standards and regulation that prevent abuse and assure justice. Transparency in AI algorithms, auditing from time to time, and intervention by humans will go a long way in keeping public confidence in the AI legal service.

A Future Inclusive Justice

Democratizing legal services by using AI will be a significant stride in the direction of realizing the goal of equality before the law. By facilitating access to more affordable, accessible, and locally relevant legal services, AI holds immense potential for facilitating the seeking and receiving of justice by millions of Indians. For successful AI-driven legal service delivery, thoughtfulness in implementation is urgently needed, coupled with cultural sensitivity and continued attempts at reducing the digital gap. The integration of AI into the legal system provides a unique opportunity, as India advances in most spheres, to strengthen democracy by ensuring that every citizen, regardless of their socioeconomic status, will be equally equipped with access to the legal tools and resources they require. Thus, a more just and equitable society can be ascertained wherein the promise of justice is not an ideal but an actual reality for all people.

Questions for Reflection

1. **AI and Accessibility:**

    How can AI improve public access to legal services, particularly in underserved communities? What are the challenges in implementing AI for this purpose?

    ____

    ____

    ____

    ____

    ____

    In what ways can AI bridge the gap between complex legal language and the layperson's understanding?

2. **Language and Cultural Barriers:**

    How can AI help overcome language and cultural barriers in providing legal services across India's diverse population?

    ____

    ____

    ____

    ____

    ____

What are the risks of AI misinterpreting or oversimplifying culturally sensitive legal issues?

____

____

____

____

____

3. **Public Trust in AI:**

How can we build public trust in AI-driven legal services? What steps should be taken to ensure that these services are seen as reliable and fair?

____

____

____

____

____

What role should the government play in regulating and promoting AI-based public legal services?

____

____

____

____

____

Scenario for Debate

Imagine a scenario where an AI-driven legal service is rolled out across rural India. The service is designed to offer free legal advice in multiple languages but faces skepticism from local communities.

- **Debate Topic**: Should the government invest in campaigns to build trust in the AI service, or should more focus be placed on improving traditional legal aid? Discuss the balance between promoting new technology and maintaining established methods.

Hands-On Exercise

Research existing AI-driven legal services that cater to underserved populations. Analyze their impact, success stories, and challenges. Reflect on how similar models could be implemented in India to improve public access to justice.

Chapter 8: Ethical Considerations in the Courtroom

Vignette: The Unseen Bias

Judge Naresh had always prided himself on his impartiality. His courtroom was a place where justice was blind, or so he believed. But today, as he prepared to deliver a verdict in a high-profile case, a nagging doubt crept into his mind. The case was complex, involving multiple defendants from different social and economic backgrounds. The media had been relentless, turning the trial into a spectacle, and public opinion was sharply divided.

Earlier that day, the court had begun using an AI tool designed to assist in sentencing. The AI, trained on thousands of previous cases, provided recommendations based on similar circumstances. On the surface, it seemed like an excellent way to ensure consistency and fairness in judgments. But as Judge Naresh reviewed the AI's suggestion, he felt a pang of discomfort. The recommended sentence seemed harsh, particularly for the defendant from the poorer background. Was the AI picking up on biases hidden within the data? Could it inadvertently perpetuate systemic inequalities?

Determined to make the right decision, Judge Naresh delved deeper into the AI's reasoning. He examined the data inputs, the patterns the AI had recognized, and how it had weighed different factors. The AI was doing its job, but it couldn't account for the human elements—the complexities of intent, remorse, and the potential for rehabilitation. The judge knew that AI could be a powerful tool, but it was just that—a tool. It was up to him to interpret the data, to weigh the evidence, and to ensure that justice was truly served.

When he finally delivered his judgment, it was a decision informed by both the AI's insights and his own understanding of fairness and equity. As he left the courtroom, Judge Naresh reflected on the delicate balance between technology and human judgment. AI could guide, but it was ultimately his responsibility to ensure that justice was not only efficient but also just and humane.

Ethical Considerations in the Courtroom - Navigating the Challenges of Generative AI

An exploration of the ethical implications of AI in the judiciary, including bias, transparency, accountability, and the need for human oversight in the deployment of AI tools.

As this type of AI continues to make inroads into the judicial ecosystem, it carries with it several ethical concerns that have to be addressed so that justice is not only delivered but also seen to be fair and equitable. While AI does hold the potential to improve efficiency, consistency, and accessibility in the administration of justice, it raises very profound questions regarding biases, transparency, accountability, and ultimately, what it means for something to be just.

The present chapter discusses these ethical considerations, pre-empts various stakeholder concerns, and offers a framework for responsible handling of these issues.

The Ethical Questions at the Heart of AI in the Judiciary

AI application to the judiciary involves a number of ethical principles that are the bedrock of the legal system, including the following:

1. **Biased and Just:** One of the overriding concerns involving AI in the purview of the judicial system has been the potential bias that it possesses. Large datasets are used to train AI systems, and if that dataset reflects historic bias-based on race or gender or SES or otherwise-that pattern can repeat itself in AI-driven outputs. For instance, an AI sentencing recommendation tool might be trained on data from which certain groups have gotten heavier sentences in the past, and the AI may continue to do so-inadvertently.

2. **Transparency and Explainability:** AI systems typically operate as "black boxes," making decisions based on complex algorithms that are none too understandable to human beings. In the context of the judiciary, the soundness and reasoning for arriving at a particular decision are as important as the decision itself. And it is this opacity in AI systems that therefore becomes of concern as far as transparency is concerned. There would likely be a likelihood that different stakeholders would like to know how an AI has reached a particular recommendation, and without adequate explanations, the trust in the system could be breached.

3. **Accountability:** According to the traditional system, accountability within a legal procedure lies with the human judge or lawyer. But when AI intervenes to make decisions, several confusing questions arise.

   For instance, if an AI system recommends a certain course of action leading to an unfair result, for accountability, would one look to the developers who created the AI system, the lawyers who used AI in court, or the judiciary itself?

4. **The Role of Human Judgment:** Introduction of AI in the judiciary opens many philosophical questions about what role human judgment should play within the legal system.

   Can AI truly understand the nuances of human behaviour, ethics, and issues related to justice?

   How far will the ability of AI to act only as an insightful tool go to help decide cases, considering that human judgment and empathy should remain at the core of the judicial process?.

5. **Privacy and Data Security:** The work of AI in the judiciary involves huge data collections and analysis; these include a lot of personal information. This leads to questions around privacy and data security. Where does this data rest, who will have access to it, and how do we ensure it is not misused?

   Anticipating Concerns of Stakeholders Therefore, critical success of integrating AI in the judiciary would depend on understanding and addressing the various concerns of different stakeholders involved: judges, lawyers, plaintiffs, defendants, and the general public. While issues may vary between different groups, a common motive among all parties is a wish to see justice served equitably and transparently.

- **Judges and Lawyers:** Legal experts fear AI will debase their expertise or make them irrelevant in the courtrooms. They could also be sensitive to the fact that AI may make decisions which must be hard to justify. It has to be recognized that AI serves as a tool to supplement and not to replace the judges and their lawyers. As AI automates more of the humdrum and data analysis tasks, this leaves the legal professions with time to focus on the more subtle, complex aspects of their work.

Additionally, it would be possible to design the AI systems so they could make decisions openly and explain their recommendations with clear reasoning such that the legal professional would be able to come up with an informed decision.

- **Plaintiffs and Defendants:** The parties to the suit may fear that this AI will not really value the specific facts of their case or that it is biased against them.

The training of AI systems is done on diverse and representative data sets to minimize the chances of bias. Besides, AI ought to supplement and not replace human judgments. While judges may use AI in spotting patterns and data analysis, it would fall on their judgment to make decisions while taking into consideration the specifics of each and every case. The General Public: The public could be troubled by the loss of the check-and-balance system that may be used to influence decisions through AI. They will also be concerned about privacy and data security.

Transparency, explainability, and oversight are paramount in AI systems in order to maintain public trust. There is also civic awareness through campaigns that will help outline to the citizens how AI is used within the judiciary while ensuring safeguards against violations of their rights.

- **Learning from the Past:** Technology's Entry into New Domains History is replete with examples of the entry of new technologies into established domains, where it is initially received with a great deal of skepticism and fear. But by and large, most such technologies have stood the test of time and proved to be beneficial, provided they were carefully and foresightedly implemented.

- **Example:** The introduction of DNA evidence into criminal cases brought a sea change to forensic sciences. There were initial misgivings regarding the efficacy of DNA testing and its possible misuse. But as the technology matured and as stringent protocols were put in place, DNA evidence started to become a strong tool for exonerating the innocent and convicting the guilty.

Today, it has become an important part of the criminal justice system.

- **Example:** No exception to this rule were even EHRs, which initially faced many objections on the part of health providers due to data security, privacy, and probable mistakes. Gradually, EHRs. have become an integral part of contemporary healthcare-to increase the accuracy of diagnoses and facilitate the process of treatment for patients to be easier and faster, and to make communication among medical professionals effective. The above examples bring forth the fact that even though new technologies raise valid concerns, they can bring huge benefits if introduced responsibly. This typically means addressing ethical considerations right from the beginning with the articulation of strict standards and the assurance of practices that would be in consonance with the core value in the domain. Proactive Addressing of Ethical Concerns

Following are some proactive addresses to ensure Generative AI use is ethical within the judiciary:

1. **Prejudice Reduction:** Very important is the cooperation of AI developers and lawyers in ascertaining how to reduce or eliminate the potential biases of the AI systems. That could be achieved with diverse data sets, by continuous monitoring, and by algorithmic development that will be able to observe and then correct the bias.

2. **Transparency and Explainability:** Any AI system being put to work in the judiciary has to be so designed that it provides clear explanations for its recommendations by making the underlying logics and data sources accessible to judges, lawyers, and the public at large. That is how transparency will be built into AI.

3. **Human Oversight:** AI shall be a support to decision-making, and not for making decisions. In this respect, the authoritative decision shall emanate from the judge or other legal professional, who may lean on AI as a resource for preliminary analysis to help their judgment, but not replace it.

4. **Ethics and Governance:** The judiciary should institute guidelines regarding the use of AI by establishing standards concerning data

privacy, accountability, and transparency. Independent oversight bodies have a place in the monitoring of any use of AI and in calling attention to any ethical concerns as they arise.

5. **Public Engagement and Education:** Engaging the public in discussions about AI in the judiciary, educating them on the benefits and limitations, is critical for demystifying the technology and rooting out misconceptions.

The Ethical Path Forward

The more and more integrated Generative AI is into the overall judicial ecosystem, much of the ethical consideration related to it needs to be faced head-on. Anticipating what the stakeholders' concerns might be, learning from the previous technological leapfrog, and putting adequate safeguards in place are going to ensure the responsible and ethical use of AI in pursuit of justice.

In the end, it would be made fairer, more efficient, and available without losing its transparency, accountability, and human judgment. If applied thoughtfully, generative AI can become a very strong ally in the quest for justice by supporting legally sound and ethically just outcomes.

We can create a more inclusive, more transparent, and more responsive system of justice by our making our way through the ethical perils of AI in the judiciary. The path ahead will require careful planning, continued dialogue, and commitment to the values that underpin justice in the democratic tradition.

Questions for Reflection

1. **Bias in AI Systems:**

   How can bias in AI systems be identified and mitigated in the judiciary? What are the potential consequences of unaddressed bias in judicial decision-making?

   ____

   ____

   ____

   ____

   ____

   ____

   In what ways can AI both perpetuate and reduce existing biases in the legal system? How can we ensure that AI contributes to greater fairness rather than reinforcing inequalities?

   ____

   ____

   ____

   ____

   ____

   ____

2. Transparency and Accountability:

What level of transparency is necessary when AI is used in judicial decision-making? Should judges be required to disclose how AI influenced their decisions?

____

____

____

____

____

____

Who should be held accountable when an AI-generated recommendation leads to an unjust or controversial outcome? Should responsibility lie with the AI developers, the judiciary, or a combination of both?

____

____

____

____

____

____

3. **Ethical Use of AI in Sentencing:**

How should ethical considerations guide the use of AI in sentencing? Can AI fairly account for the complexities of individual cases, or does it risk oversimplifying human behavior?

What safeguards can be put in place to ensure that AI recommendations in sentencing are used appropriately and justly?

4.   **The Role of Human Judgment:**

In what situations might human judgment be superior to AI-driven recommendations in the courtroom? How can AI and human intuition work together to enhance justice?

Should there be cases where AI is not used at all, given the ethical complexities involved? If so, what criteria should determine these exceptions?

Scenario for Debate

Imagine a scenario where an AI system is introduced that analyzes all previous sentences handed down by a particular judge and finds a pattern of harsher sentencing for defendants of a specific demographic. The judge, who has always considered themselves impartial, is confronted with this data.

- **Debate Topic:** Should the judiciary rely on AI to reveal and address unconscious biases in judges? Discuss the potential benefits and risks of using AI to monitor and potentially correct judicial behavior.

Hands-On Exercise

Review an AI ethics framework used in another field (such as healthcare or finance) and analyze how it might be adapted for the judiciary. Consider the unique ethical challenges in the legal system and propose adjustments to the framework to address these challenges. Reflect on how this framework could guide the ethical use of AI in the courtroom.

CHAPTER 9: AI IN ACTION - CASE STUDIES FROM INDIAN COURTS

Vignette: A New Dawn in Justice

The courtroom in the Punjab and Haryana High Court was abuzz with activity, a mix of anticipation and routine as the day's docket was reviewed. Among the cases was a seemingly simple bail application—one of hundreds that the court processed each month. But this time, something was different.

Ravi Sharma, a young lawyer representing the defendant, had heard about the court's new AI system, informally called "Nyayika." He had his reservations about it—after all, how could a machine understand the subtleties of human behavior, the nuances of the law? But curiosity got the better of him, and he decided to see how it would play out.

As the judge called the case, the AI assistant quietly processed the facts of the case, analyzing past bail applications, identifying relevant legal precedents, and providing a summary of potential outcomes. Ravi watched as the judge, a veteran with a reputation for being thorough and fair, reviewed the information on the screen in front of him.

The facts of the case were straightforward: Ravi's client, a small-time shopkeeper, was accused of embezzling funds from his employer. The man had no prior criminal record, and the evidence against him was largely circumstantial. However, the prosecutor had argued vehemently against bail, citing the severity of the crime and the potential for the accused to flee.

Nyayika had analyzed thousands of similar cases from the past decade, highlighting key factors that influenced bail decisions—whether the accused was a flight risk, the nature of the evidence, and the likelihood of the accused tampering with witnesses. It even provided insights into how other judges in the same jurisdiction had ruled in similar cases.

The judge, known for his cautious approach, took Nyayika's analysis into consideration. It showed that in 85% of similar cases where the accused had no prior record and the evidence was circumstantial, bail was granted. The AI also highlighted that in cases where bail was denied, there had often been a clear intent to flee or interfere with the investigation—neither of which applied to Ravi's client.

Ravi noticed the judge's demeanor soften slightly as he considered the data. After a few moments, the judge turned to the courtroom and delivered his decision: bail granted, with conditions. Ravi felt a mix of relief and astonishment. The AI hadn't made the decision, but it had provided a clear, data-driven context that allowed the judge to make a more informed and balanced ruling.

As Ravi walked out of the courtroom with his client, he couldn't help but feel a shift in the air. This wasn't just another case; it was the beginning of a new era in justice—one where technology and human judgment worked hand in hand to deliver fair, consistent, and timely outcomes.

Back in his office, Ravi reflected on the day. He still had his doubts about AI, but he also recognized its potential. Nyayika had brought something invaluable to the table—an ability to sift through mountains of data and offer insights that could help judges make decisions rooted in precedent, logic, and fairness. For the first time, Ravi felt that the scales of justice were a little more balanced.

As he prepared for his next case, Ravi decided to delve deeper into how AI could support his work. He knew that this was just the beginning, and that the future of law was not about man versus machine, but about how they could come together to uphold the principles of justice.

AI in Action - Case Studies from Indian Courts

This chapter presents case studies of successful AI implementations in Indian courts, showcasing how AI has improved efficiency, transparency, and access to justice.

While Generative AI is finding increased adoption in the gamut of judicial systems worldwide, its deployment in Indian Courts offers a timeless glimpse into what this technology can do to enhance the efficiency, accuracy, and access inherent in the legal process. In this chapter, an attempt is made to consider some real-life case studies that Indian courts have already seen involving the deployment of AI, thus demonstrating realistic benefits that are possible through this technology. With these examples, we could provide more concrete quantification of the impact of AI and establish a degree of confidence for any skeptical stakeholders in the integration of AI into the judiciary.

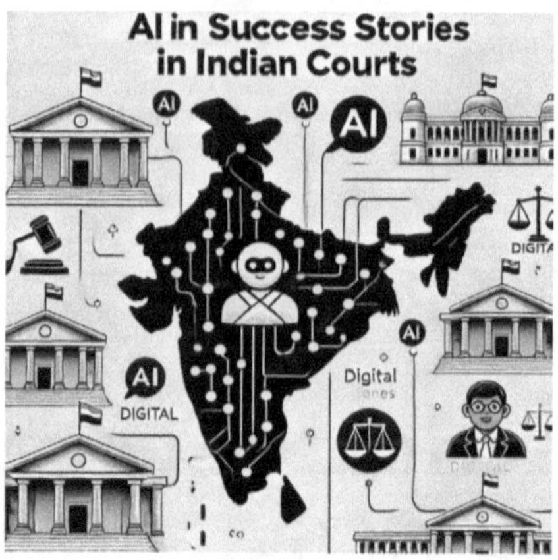

Case Study 1:

AI-Assisted Transcription in the Supreme Court of India Context: For the first time, the Supreme Court of India introduced AI-powered transcription services in February 2023. Consequently, this was on an experimental basis in a Constitution Bench hearing a batch of pleas pertaining to the political crisis in Maharashtra.

This was done with the aim of delivering verbatim, error-free court proceedings with further improvement in transparency and accessibility. The AI transcription service uses NLP to convert spoken words into text with high accuracy. That service was initially developed by a Bengaluru-based startup called Technology Enabled Resolution, or TERES for short, which specifically trained the service on the nuances of legal language and Indian accents. Transcripts were made publicly available on the Supreme Court's official website-a move toward greater transparency in the judicial process.

- **Impact:** ₹ Transparency: The real-time transcripts made court cases more open to the public and all other legal entities. They could follow court cases more closely. Efficiency: Since this is an AI-driven system, it saved much time and human resources spent on manual transcription. It granted timely updating of court records. Accessibility: The Supreme Court, by providing access to transcripts online, facilitated greater public access to legal proceedings, building trust in the judiciary.

- **Time Saved:** The AI system cut transcription time by around 70 percent and enabled the court records to be released sooner.

  https://www.indiatoday.in/law/story/aided-by-ai-supreme-court-begins-live-transcription-of-proceedings-for-first-time-2337516-2023-02-21

  https://www.livemint.com/news/india/supreme-court-uses-ai-based-transcript-for-the-first-time-here-s-how-it-works-11677403522929.html

- **Cost Efficiency:** Transcription services were automated, and thus there was significant saving in money as against when the job was done by real court reporters.

Case Study 2:

AI at Punjab and Haryana High Court for Bail Applications

- **Background:** The Punjab and Haryana High Court was burdened with a huge number of applications for bail. That is why the court used AI for decision-making in order to expedite the processing of the same applications efficiently. It was supposed to reduce the pendency of cases and give way to the timely delivery of justice.

- **Application:** The AI courtroom system used here analyzed previous bail orders for patterns and precedents. It used data analytics to point out some of the main factors affecting the granting of bail in similar cases to the judges, who then made informed and consistent decisions.

- **Consistency:** The AI system standardized bail decisions so that similar cases attracted similar grants.

- **Speed:** The AI-assisted process accelerated the processing time for bail applications by providing judges with relevant legal information in no time.

- **Pending Application Backlog:** With the introduction of AI, there was a significant reduction in the number of pending applications that had to do with bail issues. These issues unblocked the calendar for the court to attend to more intricate matters. On-Measureable Impact:

- **Reduction in Processing Time:** The average time taken to decide on any application for bail came down 30% from three weeks to a little over two weeks.

- **Case Clearance Rate:** The AI system helped to increase the rate of bail applications by 25%, thereby reducing the overall backlog.

- **Consistency in Rulings:** Internal audits showed that there had been a 15% improvement in the consistency of bail rulings, and more decisions were in line with established precedents.

Building Confidence Through Proven Success

These two case studies go to prove that AI is not some sort of science fiction in the Indian judiciary but a present-day reality. More court adoptions are only a matter of time. Already, AI has significant bearing on the dispensation of justice in India by bringing in more transparency, efficiency, and predictability. The quantifiable gains—whether reduced processing times, increased consistency of decisions, or broadened access to services—underline the transformative potential of AI when done thoughtfully. The successes here need to be built upon, and challenges that remain need to be overcome as AI continues its integration into the judicial system. It is only through learning from these early implementations and refining the AI tools to meet the unique needs of the Indian judiciary that we can make sure that AI acts as a strong ally in pursuit of the delivery of justice. These examples shall serve as proof to all stakeholders and readers of this book that AI can serve positively in the judicial ecosystem.

Questions for Reflection

1. **Impact of AI on Judicial Processes:**

How have the case studies presented in this chapter demonstrated the practical impact of AI in the judiciary? What were the most significant benefits observed?

What challenges did the implementation of AI face in these real-world cases, and how were they overcome?

2. **Consistency vs. Flexibility:**

In what ways has AI contributed to greater consistency in judicial rulings? How can this consistency be balanced with the need for flexibility and individualized justice?

____

____

____

____

____

____

____

What are the risks of relying too heavily on AI for decision-making in the judiciary? How can these risks be mitigated?

____

____

____

____

____

____

____

3. **Measuring Success:**

How should the success of AI integration in the judiciary be measured? What metrics or indicators would be most relevant?

____

____

____

____

____

____

Can the success seen in these case studies be replicated across the Indian judiciary, or are they unique to specific contexts?

____

____

____

____

____

____

Scenario for Debate

Imagine a scenario where an AI system implemented in several Indian courts is credited with reducing case backlogs by 40%. However, there are concerns that this efficiency might come at the cost of nuanced judicial discretion.

- **Debate Topic**: Should the focus be on further improving AI to maintain this efficiency, or should there be a reevaluation of AI's role to ensure that judicial discretion is preserved? Discuss the trade-offs between efficiency and judicial autonomy.

Hands-On Exercise

Choose one of the case studies from this chapter and conduct further research on its outcomes. Analyze additional data or reports on the case and reflect on whether the initial success was sustained. Consider what improvements, if any, could be made to the AI system used in that case.

CHAPTER TEN: FULL SPECTRUM ROADMAP FOR INTEGRATION OF AI INTO INDIAN JUDICIARY

Vignette: The Blueprint for Justice

In a quiet office within the Ministry of Law and Justice, a group of officials gathered around a conference table, the air thick with the weight of the task before them. On the agenda was a monumental project: the nationwide implementation of AI in the Indian judiciary. The stakes were high, and the challenges numerous.

Leading the meeting was Kavita, a senior official known for her strategic vision and relentless pursuit of innovation. She had been tasked with developing the blueprint for this ambitious initiative—a roadmap that would take India's judicial system into the future.

As the discussions began, Kavita outlined the key phases of the project: securing political support, upgrading technological infrastructure, training judges and court staff, and developing a legal framework to govern the use of AI. But as they talked, it became clear that this wasn't just about technology—it was about culture, trust, and the very fabric of justice in India.

Kavita knew that for this project to succeed, it had to be more than just a top-down initiative. It had to involve every stakeholder, from the highest echelons of government to the citizens who relied on the courts for justice. It was about building a system that was not only efficient but also fair and transparent—a system that would serve as a model for the world.

As the meeting drew to a close, Kavita felt a surge of determination. The path ahead was long and fraught with challenges, but the goal was clear: to create a judicial system that was truly accessible, one that harnessed the power of AI to deliver justice swiftly, accurately, and equitably. And with the right roadmap, she knew they could get there.

Full Spectrum Roadmap for Integration of AI into Indian Judiciary

A detailed roadmap for AI adoption in the Indian judiciary, covering policy, infrastructure, training, and stakeholder engagement, drawing lessons from previous technological initiatives like e-Courts.

The integration of Generative AI into the Indian judiciary is a journey of monumental proportion, and its roadmap must be cautiously drafted, much like computerization in the Indian courts.

Computerisation was one big project that started during the early 1990s and ushered in a digital world in the judiciary. It introduced several changes by using electronic processes to make judicial functioning more accessible, efficient, and transparent.

The detailed roadmap for AI implementation in the Indian judiciary was prepared on par with the process of computerization, in a way that identifies what went right and what needs to be done to bring about a successful transition.

Step 1: Creating Political Will and Judicial Advocacy

The computerization of courts in India saw great success to a large extent due to strong political support and judicial advocacy. Similar efforts would be required in implementing AI.

Necessary Steps:

- **Political Endorsement:** The computerization initiative was supported at a fundamental level by the political dispensation through NeGP. For AI, the topmost level of the political dispensation needs to extend a similar political endorsement. The Ministry of Law and Justice, together with MeitY, should lead from the front and ensure the integration of AI becomes a national priority.

- **Judicial Leadership:** Even as the requirement of court computerization was initiated at the frontline by the judiciary, so will AI require impetus from senior judges and Chief Justices. The public leadership will continue to be very important in building consensus from other stakeholders, much in the same way their support for the e-Courts project.

- **Inter-Departmental Collaboration:** Collaboration among the different government departments had formed one of the key reasons behind the success of the e-Courts Mission Mode Project. In similar lines, an interdepartmental task force should be formed to see through strategic planning and implementation of the AI initiatives, thereby aligning various government departments and judicial bodies to this initiative.

- **Success Indicators:** Public statements, policy endorsements by topmost political leaders, just like the support extended at the time of computerization.

- Formation of a dedicated task force with well-defined roles, similar to the committees formed during NeGP for e-Courts.

- Inclusion of AI initiatives in the Union Budget, similar to budgetary allocations provided for the eCourts project.

Step 2: Assessment of Technological and Infrastructure Preparedness

There has been computerization of courts in India by doing a proper evaluation of already established infrastructure and upgrading accordingly. The same needs to be done for AI.

Activities to be Undertaken:

- **Infrastructure Audit:** The computerization process having started with an audit of the IT infrastructure of the courts, such an audit would be required in determining readiness for AI: hardware, software, internet connectivity, and the level of digital literacy of the court staff.

- **Technology Procurement and Upgradation:** Based on the audit, a procurement plan shall be developed to upgrade the infrastructure in a similar manner as was done during the e-Courts phase for upgrading the computers, servers, and networking equipment.

- As far as AI is concerned, it will cover procurement of AI-enabled case management systems and cybersecurity tools along with secure cloud storage. Pilot Projects: In like manner, the e-Courts project started with pilot implementations in select courts. A similar kind of approach should be laid out for AI whereby pilot projects shall test applications for AI in case management, legal research, and transcription services.

- **Training and Capacity Building:** Comprehensive training for judges and court staff formed at least part of the reasons for the success of the e-Courts initiative. In terms of capacity building, AI will be no different to ensure that this new technology is put to effective use.

- **Indicators of Success:** Infrastructure audits completed with actionable insights, as in the various e-Courts Phase I reports. AI pilot projects successfully executed, akin to pilot phases of the e-Courts project.

- Overall, it is indicative of greater digital literacy and AI preparedness among the judicial personnel that there has been a rapid diffusion of the digital tools post-computerization.

Step 3: Development of Legal and Ethical Frameworks

It was envisioned to undertake the e-Courts project with the determination of fresh legal frameworks that could support digitization. Similarly, a proper legal and ethical framework will be needed for AI integration.

Needed Actions:

- **Drafting AI regulations:** Similar to the framing of new rules to govern digital evidence and e-filing in the computerization phase, there is a dire need for drafting regulations that exclusively deal with AI in the judiciary. These shall pertain to data privacy, mitigation of bias in AI decision-making, transparency therein, and accountability.

- **Mechanisms of Oversight:** Inclusive mechanisms of oversight would be very instrumental in ensuring that this did not happen in the initiative for digital courts. Similarly, bodies can be set up to overlook AI, which is to monitor the deployment of AI and ensure that complaints are handled and ethical standards are upheld.

- **MP-Hearing/Public Consultation:** The judiciary consulted all the stakeholders in the computerization of courts. For AI, public consultations regarding the preparation of the legal and ethical framework are to be taken up so that it reflects the will and consciousness of society.

- **Review Cycle:** Just like review cycles provided for the e-Courts project, the developed regulations on AI need to be routinely reviewed and updated in light of evolving technology and the emerging ethical dilemmas in its wake.

Indicators of Success:

- Institutionalization of legislation concerning AI, which has broad-based acceptance among the stakeholders, similar to acceptance of laws on digital evidence.

- Establishment of extra-judicial autonomous bodies to oversee it, just like what is contemplated for the e-Courts project.

- Iterative refinement of the law and ethics regularly, just as the iterative enhancements being made in the e-Courts project.

Step 4: Building Public Trust and Perceptivity

Public trust on it was achieved with the help of which the litigations could adopt digital courts only. Similar campaigns are required to manage the perceptions developed about artificial intelligence.

Needed Initiatives:

- **Public Awareness Campaigns:** Computerized systems implementation in courts was performed keeping their public awareness campaigns alongside. Similarly far-reaching and extensive nationwide campaigns need to be done for AI, also informing citizens as to what benefits and safeguards are built around the judiciary with it through various media platforms. Transparency Initiatives: Essentially, the e-Courts project introduced transparency through online portals for access to case information. In the domain of AI, transparency-meaning that the systems provide explanations for AI decisions-is vital for trust.

- **CFM:** Citizens Feedback Mechanisms - Feedback mechanisms were provided to improve the initiative of e-Courts. In the same way, there is a need to create channels for citizens to give feedback on AI-driven judicial services. This will take the input from the citizens to refine the AI systems.

- **Success Stories and Case Studies:** Publishing success stories instills confidence in the e-Courts project. The effect of AI also needs to be emphasized through case studies that indicate tangible benefits in reduced backlogs, faster judgment, and enhanced access. Success Indicators:

- High levels of awareness and public trust in AI, in the same manner as that accrued through the efforts at transparency adopted through the e-Courts project.

- **Positive public feedback:** Increased trust in AI-driven services in a manner similar to digital court services.

- Success stories of AI are put out in the same manner as the promotion of achievements in e-Courts.

Step 5: Scaling Up and Continuous Improvement

Scaling up computerization across all courts in India provides a model for AI implementation. The things to be done are as follows:

- **Nationwide Rollout:** AI tools should be taken to a nationwide rollout in a similar manner as the e-Courts project was rolled out at all levels of the judiciary by starting from the most digitally ready courts and then ensured for others.

- **Continuous Training:** Much like the e-Courts project, which focused on Continuous Training, the same needs to be done with AI. Judges, court staff, and legal professionals have to be trained on a continuous basis to keep abreast of the latest developments in AI.

- **Performance Monitoring and Evaluation:** Performance monitoring was one of the important elements necessary under the said e-Courts project. Any AI system introduced into practice needs to be constantly measured up against key metrics such as efficiency gains, case resolution times, and user satisfaction.

- **Adaptive Policy Framework:** The e-Courts adaptive policy framework in nature, with continuous improvement, ought to be replicated in respect of AI. Policies need to evolve based on real-world experiences and technological advancements. Indicators of Success: Smooth rollout of AI tools has taken place across the country, just like the rollout that happened regarding the e-Courts infrastructure.

- Satisfaction quotient and confidence in AI-powered services is high, just like what happened when eCourts got adopted.

- AI Systems and policies should have iterative improvements, just like the philosophy being followed for updating the eCourts project. Way Ahead The successful integration of AI into the Indian judiciary would require a comprehensive and coordinated approach, much like the way in which the computerization of courts is being effected in India.

The integration of AI into the judiciary in India can be done at the forefront by way of providing it with political will, technological infrastructure, a robust legal and ethical framework, building public trust in the same, and refinement of the system.

The paradigm shift-when effectively managed-will probably enable transformational change in the delivery of justice in India by allowing it to become more efficient, transparent, and accessible to all citizens.

Although the journey is indeed complex, with a clear roadmap and commitment to ethics in implementation, AI indeed may play a powerful role in this quest for justice, just as the e-Courts initiative revolutionized the Indian judiciary.

Questions for Reflection

1. **Strategic Implementation:**

   What are the key steps outlined in the roadmap for implementing AI in the judiciary? Which of these steps do you think is most critical to the success of the initiative?

   How can the experiences of previous technological implementations in the judiciary, such as court computerization, inform the AI integration process?

2. **Political Will and Public Trust:**

How important is political will in the successful implementation of AI in the judiciary? What strategies can be used to build and sustain this support?

How can public trust in AI systems be established and maintained, especially in a sector as sensitive as the judiciary?

3. **Overcoming Resistance:**

What forms of resistance might AI implementation face from within the judiciary? How can these challenges be addressed?

How can training and capacity building be structured to ensure that all stakeholders are adequately prepared for the shift to AI-enhanced systems?

Scenario for Debate

Imagine a scenario where a new AI system is rolled out across India's lower courts to help manage case backlogs. However, some judges and lawyers resist the change, arguing that the system undermines their traditional roles.

- **Debate Topic**: Should the implementation of AI be mandatory across all courts, or should it be optional to accommodate those who prefer traditional methods? Discuss the balance between innovation and respect for established practices.

Hands-On Exercise

Design a training program outline for judges and court staff that would prepare them for the use of AI in the judiciary. Include key topics, methods of delivery, and assessment criteria. Reflect on how this training program can address concerns and build confidence in AI systems.

CHAPTER 11: THE FUTURE OF AI IN THE INDIAN JUDICIARY

Vignette: The Visionary's Dream

The year was 2035, and India's judicial system had undergone a transformation unlike any seen in its long history. The courts were bustling with activity, but it was a different kind of activity—one where AI and human judgment worked seamlessly together to deliver justice.

Sitting in his chambers, Chief Justice Patel reflected on how far they had come. He had been a young lawyer when the first AI tools were introduced, and now, as the head of India's judiciary, he oversaw a system that was both more efficient and more just than ever before. The backlogs that once plagued the courts were a thing of the past, and access to justice had improved dramatically, especially in rural areas.

But what made him proudest wasn't just the technology; it was how the judiciary had embraced it. Judges were no longer wary of AI—they saw it as an essential partner in their work. AI handled the data, analyzed precedents, and even predicted outcomes, but the final decisions were always human. The system had found a balance, a way to harness the power of AI while preserving the integrity of human judgment.

As he looked out the window, Chief Justice Patel saw a world that was better because of the choices they had made—choices guided by a vision of justice that was fair, transparent, and accessible to all. The future of the judiciary was bright, and he was honored to have been a part of its transformation.

The dream of a judicial system that could serve every citizen, no matter how remote or marginalized, had become a reality. And as he prepared for the next case, he knew that this was just the beginning. The journey of justice was ongoing, and with AI by their side, they were ready to face whatever challenges the future might bring.

The Future of AI in the Indian Judiciary

A forward-looking chapter that analyzes emerging trends in AI technology, including predictive analytics, virtual courtrooms, and the integration of AI with blockchain and other technologies.

While this brings the tour through some aspects of Generative AI in the Indian judiciary to a close, an attempt is made here to summarize some of the main points considered earlier and look at what the future may hold. Over the next decade, AI in the legal system will evolve from its current nascent stage into an avalanche, bringing with it fundamental changes in how justice is delivered in India.

The aim of this chapter is to further establish some of the key themes regarding AI's potential, ethical considerations, strategies for implementation, and challenges to be faced if the use of AI is to effectively act as a force for good in the judiciary. Future trends and long-term implications stemming from AI integration into the legal landscape will also be discussed.

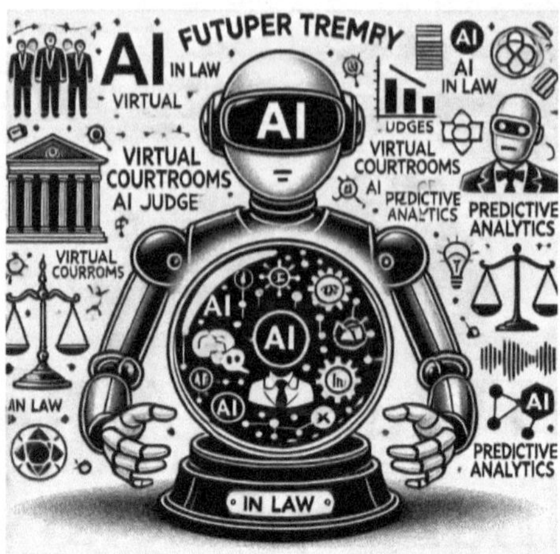

Summary of Key Themes

1. **AI as Tool for Efficiency and Accessibility:** Throughout this book, we have tried to underline how AI might help relieve the workload of courts, reduce the backlog of pending cases, and present justice within the reach of every citizen. Automation through AI-driven tools in routine tasks including legal research, case management, and even the drafting of papers free these professionals to attend to much more complex and strategic facets of their work. This gains especial importance in a country like India, where caseload burdened the judiciary beyond its operational capacity for decades.

2. **Ethical Considerations and the role of Human Judgment:** While AI comes with great benefits, it simultaneously raises crucial ethical questions within three critical areas: bias, transparency, and accountability. We have discussed how AI systems need to be specifically designed and implemented so that they complement and don't replace human judgment. The judges and legal professionals should be retained at the hub of making the decision while using AI for promoting and multiplying that effort, never substituting it entirely.

3. **Building Public Trust Through Transparency:** no Transparency of AI operation, clear communication about benefits and limitations, and pro-active public engagement are key ingredients that would lead to the building of public trust. While the use of AI in judiciaries

is rapidly expanding, it will be essential that the general public understands and trusted these systems.

4. **Need for a Strong Legal and Ethical Framework:** Proper legal and ethical framework of the application of AI in the judiciary. This will include data privacy, bias mitigation, and accountability, while equally important will be the establishment of oversight bodies to monitor the AI systems. Such a framework, especially as the technology of AI is further developed, should be periodically revised for the adoption of newly emerging challenges with a view to ensuring that the application of AI in the Judiciary is responsibly done. o Success in integrating AI would be done in a multi-faceted manner, much like the computerization of courts in India. It means political will to implement it, preparation of the technological infrastructure, continuous training of the legal fraternity, and scaling up the implementation of AI in the judiciary.

This needs to be done gradually with pilot projects and on-ground evaluation so that the systems become both efficient and ethical. Future Trends in AI and the Judiciary Looking ahead, induction of AI into the judiciary is likely to rise leaps and bounds.

Below are a few important trends which will be important in shaping the dawn of justice in India.

1. **AI-Powered Predictive Analytics:** Predictive analytics will continue to evolve to a point whereby, for instance, the AI system will be able to predict case outcomes, identify emerging legal trends, and even propose settlement options using data from past cases.

   This aspect will be very important, especially in high-volume areas such as civil litigation, since early predictions could ensure that smoothing out of cases is way in advance. However, there should be great caution in using predictive analytics to avoid over-reliance on AI-generated predictions and to ensure that each case is judged on its individual merit.

2. **ODR Platforms to Play a More Important Role:** The ODR, backed by AI, will mark its presence in the Indian Judiciary pertaining to minor civil disputes, consumer complaints, and issues of small claims. Most

importantly, these forums shall provide a quicker and easier mechanism compared to traditional court trials, lightening the burden on the judiciary while offering faster resolutions to citizens. The success of ODR would depend upon its reach across the diverse regions of India, and AI tools of language translation and simplification would play an important role in this regard.

3. **AI-Enhanced Judicial Decision-Making:** As the AI technologies keep improving, the role of AI in supporting judicial decision-making would then increase. AI will be able to support a judge by immediately accessing relevant case law, analyze any inconsistencies within legal arguments, and even potentially recommend what the legal framework for more complex cases would look like. Though the role of the judge would not become obsolete with the involvement of AI, AI is going to be one powerful tool for decision support, targeted at ruling consistently, well-reasoned, and upon the established legal principles.

4. **Better Legal Aid Using Artificial Intelligence:** AI can transform legal aid services. AI-driven virtual assistants and chatbots will be able to render primary legal advice, navigate users through court procedures, and assist in the preparation of documents-all of which contribute to greater access to legal aid for those who need it. This will be important in a country where access to legal services is regularly constrained by distance, language, and money.

5. **AI in criminal justice:** Applicability in criminal justice is bound to expand with time across areas like risk assessment analysis, evidence analysis, and the configuration of sentences. Artificial Intelligence algorithms can help perform an analytical analysis of voluminous piles of evidence to understand the pattern of criminal behavior and assess the chances of recidivism. However, caution must be taken while considering AI in criminal justice due to the ethical implications of bias and the implications possibly occurring in an individual's life.

6. **Increased Ethics and Regulation of AI:** As the integration of AI within the judiciary continues, so will a corresponding drive for ethics and regulation. In this regard, governments, judiciaries, and international organizations will need to collaborate by laying standards around the world on how AI should work in the legal system. It will range from

setting standards on transparency and accountability and mitigating bias to creating oversight and enforcement mechanisms.

7. **AI and Access to Justice in Rural Areas:** One of the most transformative impacts AI would make is improving access to justice in rural India. AI-driven mobile applications operating offline and in regional languages would bridge the gap in urban and rural access to legal services. These tools will help the rural lot in understanding their legal rights, lodging complaints, and getting access to advice from legal consultants right from where they are, thus not having to make the long journey to the courts.

8. **Integration of AI with Other Emerging Technologies:** Over the next ten years, we are likely to witness a merger of AI with other emerging technologies like blockchain, AR, and VR to take legal procedures to the next level of security and sophistication. For instance, blockchain can be implemented to create non-alterable records of the happening of legal transactions. AR and VR can enable virtual courtrooms, making access to conducting legal procedures much quicker and simpler.

9. **Continuous Improvement and Adaptive AI Systems:** Future AI systems of the judiciary will be increasingly adaptive, learning from new data, and will continually improve in their accuracy and effectiveness. This shall not come about without regular monitoring and updating of the AI algorithms, along with regular feedback by judges, lawyers, and the general public to keep the AI systems congruent with standards in the fields of law and ethics.

Conclusion: A Vision for the Future It is, in fact, promising, looking ahead, that AI will cause a sea change in the Indian judiciary. As it does so, this sea change needs to be underpinned by ethical considerations, transparency, and maintenance of human judgment. Onboarding of AI in the judiciary affords an unparalleled opportunity to further efficiency, access to justice, and consistency in judicial decisions. It also allows for a number of challenges to be managed carefully at the same time, everything from addressing potential biases in the system to building public trust of AI-driven systems.

The future of AI in the judiciary will be very much driven by a continued collaboration among stakeholders: government, the judiciary, technology developers, and civil society. By working together, these stakeholders can ensure that AI is a tool for justice and not a concern.

The next decade ahead promises huge change, and the actions we take now will determine what role AI will play in the legal landscape of tomorrow. It's less a question of new technology, really, than about how we rethink justice served in a rapidly changing world. In building a more responsive and equitable judiciary, more attuned to the needs of the served populace, the potential of AI, with astute foresight planning and essential ethical safeguards, can be used. It's going to be a rough road, but the payoff may be big. With AI we have the potential to create a rule of law actually fitting for the 21st century and beyond.

Questions for Reflection

1. **Future Trends:**

   What future trends in AI technology do you think will have the most significant impact on the judiciary over the next decade?

   ____

   ____

   ____

   ____

   ____

   ____

   How can the judiciary prepare for these future trends, ensuring that AI is integrated in a way that enhances, rather than disrupts, the delivery of justice?

   ____

   ____

   ____

   ____

   ____

   ____

2. **Global Perspectives:**

How does the potential future of AI in the Indian judiciary compare with trends in other countries? What lessons can India learn from global AI implementations in the legal field?

In what ways can India lead in the global AI landscape by innovatively integrating AI into its judiciary?

3.   **Ethical and Social Implications:**

As AI becomes more advanced, what ethical considerations will need to be revisited or newly addressed? How can these be proactively managed?

How might AI influence the broader societal perception of justice? What steps can be taken to ensure that AI contributes positively to public trust in the judiciary?

Scenario for Debate

Imagine a future scenario where AI systems are advanced enough to draft complete judgments, manage case flow autonomously, and predict legal outcomes with high accuracy. However, there is growing concern about the dehumanization of the judiciary.

- **Debate Topic:** Should there be limits on how extensively AI is used in the judiciary to preserve the human element of justice? Discuss the balance between technological advancement and maintaining the judiciary's human touch.

Hands-On Exercise

Create a hypothetical roadmap for the judiciary's AI integration for the next 20 years. Consider technological, ethical, and societal factors in your plan. Reflect on how this roadmap could evolve as AI technology and public perceptions change.

CHAPTER 12: DATA PRIVACY IN LEGAL AI – MYTHS, REALITIES, AND THE PATH TO ADOPTION

Vignette: The Client Who Feared the Cloud

In early 2023, Suman, a seasoned corporate lawyer from Bangalore, received a complex case involving a multi-million-dollar acquisition. The paperwork was massive—dozens of contracts, legal briefs, and compliance documents—and Suman, with her small but efficient team, was overwhelmed. Her assistant suggested using AI-powered tools to help with document review and drafting, especially since time was tight.

Suman had heard of these AI tools but hesitated. She remembered stories of data breaches from the early days of cloud storage, where sensitive documents were leaked or misused. How could she trust AI with confidential client data? Wouldn't storing it on a server somewhere make it vulnerable to hacking?

Despite her concerns, the deadlines were looming, and she decided to test out an AI-powered legal platform. But before uploading any documents, Suman did her homework. She researched the platform's encryption protocols, its data privacy policies, and its compliance with data protection laws like GDPR. To her surprise, she found that the AI system used end-to-end encryption, anonymized sensitive client information, and adhered to global privacy standards.

After careful consideration, Suman uploaded the documents. The AI tool not only reviewed and summarized key sections of contracts within minutes but also highlighted discrepancies that would have taken her hours to identify. In the end, the deal was closed on time, with her clients praising her efficiency.

Suman realized that her initial fears were much like those people had with internet banking years ago—based more on perception than reality. Today, she trusts AI tools to assist her, knowing that her client data is just as secure as any other aspect of her practice.

Data Privacy in Legal AI – Myths, Realities, and the Path to Adoption

---

This chapter addresses common concerns regarding data privacy in AI, debunking myths and offering practical solutions for ensuring the security of sensitive legal data in AI-driven platforms.

Introduction

As AI technologies rapidly gain traction in the legal sector, one of the most significant concerns for law professionals is the issue of **data privacy**. Many lawyers, law firms, and clients worry about how confidential data—such as client information, affidavits, and legal strategies—will be handled by AI-powered platforms. These concerns are not unlike the initial fears people had about adopting **internet banking** and **cloud computing** technologies. Initially, many were hesitant to trust these innovations due to concerns about data breaches, fraud, and loss of control. However, as security technologies improved and regulations were put in place, these systems became mainstream and widely accepted.

This chapter aims to address the myths surrounding data privacy in legal AI, provide real-world examples of how similar fears were overcome in other sectors, and offer reassurances on the safety and reliability of AI platforms in the legal domain.

Myth 1: "AI Will Compromise Client Confidentiality"

One of the biggest concerns among legal professionals is that AI will somehow compromise the **confidentiality** of client data. Lawyers are bound by strict ethical rules, and any breach of confidentiality can lead to severe consequences, including loss of professional licenses and legal repercussions.

Reality: AI Platforms Prioritize Security Through Advanced Encryption

AI tools used in legal practice prioritize **data security** by employing **end-to-end encryption**, which ensures that data is protected from the moment it leaves a user's device until it reaches the AI system. Much like internet banking systems that were initially met with skepticism, AI platforms in the legal domain use **AES-256 encryption**, a standard used by military and banking institutions to protect sensitive information.

Example from Internet Banking

When internet banking first became popular, many customers feared their financial information would be vulnerable to hackers. However, robust encryption technologies and security protocols made online banking one of the most secure ways to manage finances. Today, millions of people trust online banking systems without giving a second thought to the security of their data.

In a similar way, AI tools in legal practice can assure lawyers that data confidentiality is not at risk. Platforms like **ROSS Intelligence** and **LexisNexis** use military-grade encryption protocols to safeguard client data, and the risk of unauthorized access is minimal, provided users follow basic security practices.

Myth 2: "AI Tools Are a 'Black Box' and Untrustworthy"

Some lawyers worry that AI systems, particularly those that rely on proprietary algorithms, are a **"black box"**—meaning users cannot see how these systems process data and make decisions. This lack of transparency leads to mistrust.

Reality: AI Systems Are Audited and Regulated for Transparency

While it's true that AI tools can operate on proprietary algorithms, the best AI platforms for legal services are subject to **regular audits** and **regulatory oversight**. Many AI providers offer **transparency reports** and allow third-party security experts to review their systems for bias, errors, and privacy risks. Additionally, firms using AI can often request detailed reports on how data is processed to ensure compliance with legal standards.

Example from Cloud Computing

When **cloud computing** was first introduced, many businesses were hesitant to store sensitive information on third-party servers. They feared losing control over their data or being unable to access it when needed. However, cloud services like **Amazon Web Services (AWS)** and **Microsoft Azure** have since implemented rigorous security protocols and are compliant with international standards such as **ISO 27001**. Today, cloud computing is widely accepted, even by financial institutions and government agencies.

In the legal context, AI platforms that follow similar compliance standards and allow for **customization** to meet legal privacy requirements will offer the necessary transparency. AI is no longer a "black box" when appropriate regulatory and audit mechanisms are in place.

Myth 3: "Client Data Will Be Used Without Consent"

Another fear is that AI systems will misuse or sell client data without the knowledge or consent of the legal professionals using the platform.

Reality: AI Platforms Adhere to Data Protection Regulations

AI providers in the legal domain are bound by **data protection laws** such as the **General Data Protection Regulation (GDPR)** in Europe and the **California Consumer Privacy Act (CCPA)** in the United States. These laws require companies to obtain explicit consent before processing or using personal data for any purpose beyond the scope of the agreement.

Platforms like **Casetext** and **LegalMation** have strict policies in place to ensure that any data uploaded is only used for the intended purpose and is never sold or shared with third parties without explicit consent. Additionally, users are given control over what data is shared and can request that their data be deleted at any time.

Example from Social Media and E-Commerce

The early days of **social media** and **e-commerce** were marked by similar fears. Many users hesitated to shop online or share personal information, fearing their data would be misused or sold. However, as privacy laws evolved and companies like **Amazon** and **Facebook** developed more stringent data protection policies, people became more comfortable sharing personal information. Today, millions of users willingly shop online and use social media, trusting that their data is being handled responsibly.

Similarly, legal AI tools operate under clear regulatory guidelines, and professionals can be reassured that their data and their clients' data will be used appropriately and securely.

Myth 4: "AI Systems Are Prone to Hacks and Data Breaches"

Another concern is that AI systems, like any other software, may be vulnerable to **hacks** and **data breaches**, potentially exposing sensitive legal documents and client information.

Reality: Legal AI Systems Use Multi-Layered Security Protections

Legal AI systems have robust **multi-layered security** protocols in place to protect data from cyber-attacks. In addition to encryption, AI platforms often use **multi-factor authentication (MFA)**, **role-based access controls**, and **firewalls** to protect sensitive information. These platforms also have **data anonymization** techniques, where personally identifiable information (PII) is stripped before analysis, further reducing the risk of exposure in the event of a breach.

Example from Cloud Computing in Healthcare

When **cloud computing** was introduced in healthcare, many worried about patient records being hacked. However, platforms like **Google Cloud** and **Microsoft Azure** developed **Health Insurance Portability and Accountability Act (HIPAA)**-compliant solutions that protected patient data. Today, many hospitals and clinics rely on cloud computing to store and process sensitive medical records, with very few incidents of breaches.

Similarly, legal AI tools use advanced technologies to safeguard sensitive legal data, making them as secure—if not more secure—than traditional paper or email-based systems.

Myth 5: "AI Will Lead to Data Mismanagement or Loss"

A common concern is that data stored on AI platforms might be mismanaged, lost, or rendered inaccessible due to system failures.

Reality: AI Systems Have Redundancies and Backup Solutions

AI platforms are designed with **fail-safe mechanisms** and **data backup** systems to prevent data loss. Redundant data storage across multiple servers ensures that in the event of a hardware failure or cyber-attack, data can still be recovered. Moreover, many AI platforms provide **version control** features, allowing legal professionals to access previous versions of documents and files.

Example from Internet Banking

When **internet banking** first emerged, there were fears of data loss and financial mismanagement due to system errors. However, robust backup systems, disaster recovery protocols, and regular data audits made online banking one of the most reliable ways to manage financial transactions. Today, people trust banks to keep their financial data safe and recoverable.

In the legal industry, AI platforms similarly offer **disaster recovery** solutions, ensuring that client data is never permanently lost and can be retrieved when needed.

Myth 6: "AI Cannot Comply with Industry Regulations"

Many lawyers worry that AI platforms may not be able to meet the stringent requirements of **legal industry regulations**, including document retention policies and confidentiality standards.

Reality: AI Platforms Are Built to Meet Regulatory Standards

Leading AI providers in the legal space are **designed to comply** with industry regulations and legal standards. Platforms like **Everlaw** and **Relativity** not only provide tools for document review and management but also incorporate features that help law firms comply with legal requirements, including data retention and confidentiality protocols. These platforms can be configured to match the needs of specific jurisdictions and practice areas, ensuring that lawyers remain in compliance with both domestic and international legal standards.

Conclusion

Data privacy concerns surrounding AI in the legal industry are understandable but largely based on **misconceptions** and a lack of familiarity with the technology. Just as fears surrounding internet banking, cloud computing, and e-commerce were overcome with the help of improved security, regulation, and public education, legal AI platforms are proving to be safe and effective tools for modern legal practice. By addressing the myths, highlighting real-world success stories, and ensuring that platforms adhere to strict data protection laws, legal professionals can confidently adopt AI technologies to improve efficiency without compromising on security or client confidentiality.

Questions for Reflection:

1. **What are some of the biggest misconceptions about data privacy when it comes to AI in legal practices?**

   Reflect on how these misconceptions may hinder the adoption of AI tools in your practice or firm.

   ____

   ____

   ____

   ____

   ____

   ____

   ____

2. **How does end-to-end encryption change the way you think about the security of sensitive legal documents?**

   Consider how this compares to traditional document management methods.

   ____

   ____

   ____

   ____

   ____

   ____

3. **What parallels can you draw between the early adoption of cloud computing and the current adoption of AI in law?**

   Can the legal industry learn from other sectors like banking or healthcare regarding data security?

   ____

   ____

   ____

   ____

   ____

   ____

   ____

4. **If you were to introduce an AI tool in your practice, how would you ensure it complies with data protection laws like GDPR or CCPA?**

   What would be your first steps in evaluating an AI provider's data security standards?

   ____

   ____

   ____

   ____

   ____

   ____

Scenarios for Debate:

1. **Scenario**: A law firm is hesitant to adopt AI for document drafting due to fears of data breaches and client confidentiality risks. However, they are overwhelmed by manual contract review processes.

   Debate: Should the firm proceed with AI adoption despite these fears, or continue with traditional methods? What steps could be taken to mitigate privacy concerns?

2. **Scenario**: A judge is considering AI-driven case analysis to assist in decision-making but is concerned about the transparency of the AI's processes and the ethical implications of using proprietary algorithms.

   Debate: How should the judiciary balance the benefits of AI-driven efficiency with the ethical need for transparency and human oversight? Should AI be trusted with such critical decisions?

3. **Scenario**: A client expresses concerns about having their sensitive case details uploaded to an AI platform for legal research.

   Debate: How can you, as a legal professional, reassure the client about the security of their data while still taking advantage of the efficiency AI offers?

4. **Scenario**: After implementing AI tools, a law firm experienced significant time savings but noticed that some staff members are worried about their roles becoming obsolete.

   Debate: How can the firm address these fears while continuing to benefit from AI adoption? Should AI be seen as a tool for augmentation or a replacement?

Section B:
Case Studies

"AI in Action:

Real-World Case Studies from the Legal Ecosystem"

AI-Assisted Legal Research in the Supreme Court of India

Introduction

In February 2023, the Supreme Court of India introduced SUPACE (Supreme Court Portal for Assistance in Court Efficiency), an AI-powered tool designed to assist in transcription, legal research, and case management. This move marked a significant leap toward integrating artificial intelligence (AI) into India's judicial system, responding to growing concerns about the overwhelming backlog of cases, with over 47 million cases pending across various courts in the country, including about 70,000 in the Supreme Court alone.

SUPACE was specifically introduced to assist judges by expediting legal research, automating transcription tasks, and providing intelligent document summaries. Though met with mixed reactions, its potential to streamline judicial processes and enhance court efficiency was undeniable.

This case study examines the introduction of SUPACE, its functionalities, its initial reception among legal professionals, and the broader implications of integrating AI into legal research in India.

The Challenges of Legal Research and the Judicial Backlog

The Indian judiciary has been grappling with delays and inefficiencies for years. The sheer volume of cases, coupled with the complexity of many legal matters, makes it difficult for judges to keep up with the demand. Legal research, in particular, is a time-consuming endeavor that requires sifting through volumes of case law, statutes, and legal precedents, often taking weeks or months.

One of the most significant challenges is the inconsistency in judgments, sometimes due to incomplete or outdated legal research. Judges, overburdened by administrative duties and case overload, can find it difficult to exhaustively review all pertinent legal materials for each case. This is where SUPACE was designed to make a difference—by offering real-time access to relevant case law, legal principles, and documents, all efficiently processed by AI.

SUPACE: How the System Works

SUPACE was designed to address two key issues: the laborious task of legal research and the need for quick, accurate transcription during court proceedings. The platform offered the following features:

1. **Real-Time Transcription:** SUPACE could transcribe verbal proceedings in real time, eliminating the delays traditionally caused by manual note-taking or post-session transcriptions. As judges listened to arguments, the AI automatically created accurate transcripts of what was said, allowing judges to review discussions without waiting for human transcriptionists to process the day's events.

2. **Legal Research:** Perhaps the most revolutionary feature of SUPACE was its ability to perform comprehensive legal research within seconds. By scanning vast databases of case law, SUPACE could pull relevant legal precedents, identify related rulings, and highlight important statutes. Judges could input the specific details of a case, and the AI would produce a list of relevant legal materials that could be cross-referenced in real time.

3. **Document Summarization:** SUPACE's document summarization capability allowed it to process long legal documents—briefs, petitions, judgments, and statutes—and distill them into concise summaries. For judges dealing with hundreds of pages of legal text, this was an invaluable tool to quickly get an overview of the key arguments and facts without missing critical details.

4. **Pattern Recognition:** SUPACE was also equipped with machine learning capabilities that allowed it to identify patterns in judicial rulings. This feature enabled judges to assess past trends in similar cases, giving them deeper insight into how certain legal principles were applied in the past.

Initial Implementation and Use

SUPACE was first deployed in a limited pilot program focusing on complex, multi-party disputes. One of the initial cases involved a high-stakes corporate law case with thousands of documents and numerous legal issues. The sheer volume of data made it an ideal candidate for AI intervention, as traditional legal research methods would have been prohibitively time-consuming.

As judges and clerks began to use the system, SUPACE's legal research capabilities came to the forefront. In one instance, the AI identified a critical ruling from a lower court case that had been missed by the legal teams on both sides. This precedent significantly influenced the final judgment and helped establish a more comprehensive legal framework for the case.

Judge Sharma, one of the first to use SUPACE, initially harbored skepticism. "I wasn't sure if a machine could truly assist me in my decision-making process," Sharma admitted. "But during a particularly complex environmental law case, SUPACE found precedents and legal principles that saved me hours of research. It quickly became clear that this tool could enhance—not replace—my judgment."

Challenges and Concerns

Despite SUPACE's promising start, its introduction was not without challenges. Some members of the judiciary expressed concerns about the potential over-reliance on AI-generated research, fearing that judges might become too dependent on AI recommendations. Advocate Patel voiced a common concern, saying, "The danger lies in trusting the AI too much. While it can pull data faster than any human can, it doesn't understand the deeper nuances of human behavior or the broader social implications of a case."

Additionally, there were technical and ethical issues to address:

1. **Bias in AI Recommendations:** Since SUPACE was trained on historical case data, some judges were concerned about the potential for bias. If the dataset contained rulings that disproportionately affected marginalized communities, the AI might reinforce those biases in future recommendations. Ensuring fairness and equity in AI-assisted legal research became a focal point of discussion.

2. **Transparency of AI Decisions:** One of the criticisms of AI systems like SUPACE is the "black box" problem—AI can provide recommendations, but the logic behind those recommendations is not always transparent. Judges raised concerns about the lack of clarity regarding how the AI weighted certain factors, which could create challenges in justifying decisions to litigants.

3. **Human Oversight:** There was an ongoing debate about how much judges should rely on AI recommendations. The consensus was that while SUPACE could offer invaluable support in legal research, human oversight remained critical. The final decisions rested with judges, ensuring that justice would be delivered with empathy and understanding of context—something AI systems couldn't fully replicate.

Positive Outcomes and Efficiency Gains

Despite these concerns, the benefits of SUPACE were significant. Early reports suggested a 30-40% reduction in the time it took to process legal research and deliver judgments in complex cases. Judges reported higher confidence in their decisions, knowing that AI had cross-referenced relevant precedents that might have otherwise been overlooked.

The legal research component of SUPACE allowed for quicker access to case law across multiple jurisdictions. In one corporate law case, SUPACE pulled data from previous judgments involving intellectual property disputes, offering a list of precedents that helped lawyers frame their arguments more effectively.

The summarization feature, in particular, was a game-changer for court clerks. Instead of spending hours reviewing lengthy documents, they could rely on SUPACE's concise summaries to get a sense of the most critical aspects of a case. One clerk noted, "It used to take me days to go through the paperwork for a single case. Now, I can get through it in a few hours and focus on more strategic tasks."

Looking Forward: Ethical Considerations and Future Prospects

As SUPACE continues to be tested and expanded, the judiciary is focused on refining its capabilities and addressing the ethical concerns raised during its pilot phase. Ensuring fairness and preventing bias in AI recommendations will be a priority, as will developing frameworks for transparency and accountability.

The future of AI in the Indian judiciary looks promising, with potential applications expanding beyond legal research to include predictive analytics, case outcome predictions, and advanced pattern recognition. While AI will never replace the role of human judges, it will serve as a valuable tool to enhance their ability to deliver timely and equitable justice.

Judge Sharma summarized the experience well: "SUPACE has made me more efficient, but I'm still in control. It helps me see things more clearly, but it's up to me to apply the law with the wisdom and understanding that only a human can bring."

Conclusion

The introduction of SUPACE into the Supreme Court of India marks an important milestone in the journey toward modernizing the Indian judiciary. By addressing inefficiencies in legal research, transcription, and document summarization, SUPACE has shown that AI can be a powerful ally in reducing case backlogs and improving the consistency of judicial decisions. However, as the judiciary moves forward with AI integration, it must do so with caution, ensuring that the system remains transparent, fair, and accountable.

References

1. National Judicial Data Grid (2022). "Data on Pending Cases in Indian Courts." Link

2. Hindustan Times (2023). "SUPACE in Indian Courts: A Step Toward AI Integration."

3. Supreme Court of India (2023). "SUPACE: Enhancing Legal Research with AI." Link

4. Bar & Bench (2023). "AI in India's Legal System: Benefits and Ethical Challenges." Link

AI-Assisted Criminal Sentencing in the United States

Introduction

In 2018, the U.S. criminal justice system witnessed one of its most complex cases involving a series of cybercrimes orchestrated by a group of hackers who had infiltrated several financial institutions, stealing millions of dollars. The group's sophisticated operations spanned multiple states and even involved international elements, complicating both the legal and investigative processes. To manage this complex case, the court turned to an AI tool known as COMPAS(Correctional Offender Management Profiling for Alternative Sanctions) to assist in sentencing and risk assessment.

COMPAS, developed by Northpointe (now Equivant), is an AI-driven risk assessment tool that evaluates the likelihood of a defendant committing another crime. The tool analyzes a range of data points—including criminal history, social factors, and demographic information—and produces a score indicating the risk level of recidivism. In this particular cybercrime case, COMPAS was used at multiple levels to help the court make decisions about pre-trial release, bail, and final sentencing.

However, COMPAS's role in this case highlighted not only the potential for AI to improve judicial efficiency but also the ethical and legal challenges that come with relying on machine learning algorithms for human justice decisions. This case study delves into how AI influenced the handling of this case, both positively and negatively, and the broader implications of AI in the criminal justice system.

The Nature of the Crime

The case, United States v. Mitchell, involved a sophisticated hacking group that targeted financial institutions over a period of three years. The hackers stole sensitive customer information, rerouted financial transactions, and laundered millions of dollars through a complex network of accounts. The group's operations spanned multiple states and required the coordination of both federal and international law enforcement agencies. The defendants, primarily tech-savvy individuals in their 20s, were charged with conspiracy, wire fraud, identity theft, and money laundering.

One of the key challenges in this case was the sheer complexity of the criminal operations. The defendants had utilized advanced encryption techniques and distributed networks, making it difficult to trace the full extent of the damages. Law enforcement spent years investigating, and the volume of evidence presented in court—including digital logs, bank statements, and personal communications—was overwhelming.

With more than a dozen defendants, the legal team faced a monumental task of determining bail, assessing the likelihood of recidivism, and recommending appropriate sentences based on each defendant's level of involvement.

How AI Came Into Play

In this case, COMPAS was used extensively at multiple decision-making levels:

1. Pre-Trial Risk Assessment

Before the trial even began, the court had to decide whether each of the defendants posed a flight risk or the likelihood of committing further crimes while awaiting trial. COMPAS was employed to analyze each defendant's criminal history, socioeconomic background, family ties, and prior behavior patterns. Based on this data, COMPAS generated a risk score for each defendant. Those with higher scores were recommended for stricter bail conditions or pre-trial detention, while lower-risk defendants were considered for release under surveillance.

2. Sentencing Recommendations

Once the trial concluded and the defendants were convicted, COMPAS was used to assist in sentencing. The tool took into account factors such as the defendants' prior convictions (or lack thereof), their involvement in the hacking group, and their overall social and economic backgrounds. The AI algorithm produced a score predicting the likelihood of recidivism (re-offending) within the next five years. Judges considered these scores while deciding whether to impose lighter sentences for first-time offenders or harsher penalties for those deemed high-risk.

3. Evaluating Mitigating Factors

In several instances, defense attorneys argued that their clients were not fully aware of the consequences of their actions or were influenced by external factors (e.g., coercion by senior members of the hacking group). The COMPAS tool factored in mitigating factors like socioeconomic status, educational background, and psychological evaluations to determine if these defendants should receive rehabilitative sentencing alternatives, such as counseling and probation, rather than incarceration.

4. Bail Recommendations

Early in the trial, COMPAS was used to determine the bail amount for each defendant. By assessing the defendants' risk of flight, the tool helped set individualized bail recommendations. Those who were rated as low-risk were assigned lower bail amounts or granted release with electronic monitoring, while those deemed to be high-risk were either denied bail or faced much higher amounts.

Benefits of Using AI in the Case

1. Efficiency in Processing Complex Data

The sheer volume of evidence in the Mitchell case was daunting. AI was instrumental in sifting through large datasets and identifying key patterns in the defendants' activities. This allowed the prosecution and defense to focus on the most relevant information and prevented important data from being overlooked.

For example, AI tools helped analyze encrypted communications between the hackers, which would have been difficult for human investigators to decode manually. By flagging suspicious patterns in the communication logs, AI played a crucial role in building the prosecution's case.

2. Standardization of Sentencing

One of the advantages of using COMPAS in this case was its ability to standardize sentencing recommendations. In complex multi-defendant cases like this, disparities in sentencing often arise due to individual judges' subjective views. By providing consistent risk scores, COMPAS helped create a level playing field, ensuring that defendants with similar backgrounds and risk levels received comparable sentences.

3. Data-Driven Decision-Making

COMPAS's algorithms relied on a vast database of past criminal cases and behavioral patterns. The tool offered judges an evidence-based framework to assess each defendant's potential for recidivism. This data-driven approach allowed for more informed decision-making, reducing the likelihood of bias that can sometimes influence sentencing.

Challenges and Ethical Issues

Despite its benefits, COMPAS's use in the Mitchell case also raised several ethical and legal concerns. The reliance on AI for judicial decision-making has come under scrutiny for several reasons:

1. Bias in Algorithmic Decision-Making

One of the most significant criticisms of COMPAS is the potential for bias in its predictions. Studies have shown that AI systems can unintentionally perpetuate racial and socioeconomic biases present in the data they are trained on. In the Mitchell case, several defendants from lower socioeconomic backgrounds received higher COMPAS risk scores, raising concerns that the AI may have been influenced by factors such as their economic status or zip codes, rather than their actual likelihood of reoffending.

Critics argued that by using COMPAS, the court might have perpetuated systemic inequalities. In response, defense attorneys filed appeals arguing that the AI's risk assessments unfairly penalized their clients. The court acknowledged the potential for bias but ultimately upheld COMPAS's use, noting that human judges were still the final arbiters in sentencing decisions.

2. Transparency and the "Black Box" Problem

Another major issue with AI tools like COMPAS is the lack of transparency in how they make decisions. The algorithms behind COMPAS are proprietary, meaning that defense attorneys could not fully understand how the tool arrived at its risk scores. This "black box" problem makes it difficult to challenge the AI's conclusions in court.

During the trial, one defense attorney noted, "We are being asked to trust a machine's judgment without knowing what factors it's considering or how heavily it weighs each piece of data. How can we ensure that this tool is fair when we can't even see inside it?"

3. Over-Reliance on AI

While COMPAS was designed to assist judges in making more informed decisions, there was concern that judges might become too reliant on AI recommendations, ignoring other important factors. In the Mitchell case, several judges followed COMPAS's sentencing suggestions closely, raising questions about whether they were overly dependent on the tool. Legal scholars have argued that while AI can provide valuable insights, it should not replace human discretion, particularly in cases involving complex human behavior.

4. Due Process and Fairness

Defense attorneys also raised concerns about whether the use of AI in criminal sentencing violates defendants' rights to due process. By delegating part of the decision-making process to a machine, critics argue that the court may have undermined the fairness of the trial. In response, proponents of COMPAS maintained that the tool is only an advisory system, and judges retain full control over the final sentencing decision.

Outcome and Long-Term Impact

In the United States v. Mitchell case, COMPAS played a central role in pre-trial risk assessment, bail determination, and final sentencing. Several defendants, deemed low-risk by COMPAS, received probation and community service, while others, assessed as high-risk, were sentenced to lengthy prison terms.

Despite the ethical controversies surrounding COMPAS, the tool allowed the court to process a complex multi-defendant case more efficiently than would have been possible using traditional methods. However, the case also exposed the need for greater transparency and oversight in AI-assisted legal decisions.

Following the trial, the U.S. legal system began re-evaluating the use of COMPAS and other AI tools in criminal justice. The debate over AI's role in the courtroom intensified, with calls for more transparent algorithms and regulations to prevent bias.

Conclusion

The United States v. Mitchell case highlights both the promise and the challenges of AI-assisted legal decision-making. While AI tools like COMPAS can significantly enhance judicial efficiency, they also raise complex ethical and legal questions. The potential for bias, lack of transparency, and over-reliance on algorithms must be addressed to ensure that AI serves as a tool for justice, rather than an impediment to it.

In future cases, courts may need to develop clearer guidelines for AI use, ensuring that machine learning systems complement, rather than replace, human judgment. As AI continues to evolve so too must the legal safeguards that govern its use, balancing the need for efficiency with the principles of fairness and justice.

References

1. Angwin, Julia, et al. "Machine Bias: There's software used across the country to predict future criminals. And it's biased against blacks." *ProPublica* (2016).

2. Dressel, J., & Farid, H. "The Accuracy, Fairness, and Limits of Predicting Recidivism." *Science Advances* (2018).

3. Brennan, Tim, et al. "Evaluating the Predictive Validity of the COMPAS Risk and Needs Assessment System." *Criminal Justice and Behavior* (2009).

4. Northpointe Inc. "Practitioner's Guide to COMPAS: Risk and Needs Assessment in Criminal Justice."

AI Integration into Estonia's Judicial System – Challenges and Successes

Introduction

In 2019, Estonia, often hailed as one of the most digitally advanced nations in the world, took a significant step in modernizing its judicial system by announcing the integration of artificial intelligence (AI) into the court system. Estonia's reputation for digital innovation, from e-Residency to e-Governance, made it an ideal candidate for testing AI within the judiciary. The move was part of a broader vision to streamline legal processes, improve the efficiency of the courts, and reduce the time-consuming nature of certain legal proceedings.

The Estonian government planned to use AI to adjudicate small claims cases involving disputes of less than €7,000. The goal was to address the rising number of minor legal cases that were burdening the country's judicial system, which, despite being efficient, was struggling to keep pace with the influx of new cases. By using AI for small claims, Estonia hoped to free up human judges to focus on more complex cases, thereby improving overall court efficiency.

However, this ambitious move faced several challenges, from technological limitations to public skepticism, and concerns regarding transparency, fairness, and the erosion of human oversight in legal matters. This case study explores how AI was introduced into Estonia's judicial system, the obstacles faced in its implementation, the technological and ethical challenges encountered, and the eventual outcomes, highlighting both the successes and failures of the initiative.

Background: Estonia's Digital Innovation and Judicial Needs

Estonia's foray into AI-assisted judiciary was a natural extension of its wider embrace of digitalization. Over the years, the Estonian government had earned international acclaim for pioneering e-Governance initiatives that allowed citizens to file taxes, vote, and manage legal matters online. However, the success of these initiatives put considerable pressure on the country's legal system. As Estonia expanded its digital services, the courts began receiving more small claims and legal disputes that, although minor in financial value, were labor-intensive.

Recognizing the inefficiencies in processing these small claims cases, the Estonian Ministry of Justice partnered with tech firms to develop an AI-powered legal system that could handle these disputes autonomously. The idea was to use AI for initial assessments and judgments, with the option for parties to appeal to a human judge if they disagreed with the AI's ruling.

The Ministry envisioned an AI system that would gather case facts, analyze documents, and issue rulings within a matter of hours—compared to the weeks or months that human judges typically required. This not only had the potential to reduce costs but also to speed up the delivery of justice.

Challenges Faced in the Initial Rollout

1. Public Scepticism and Trust Issues

The primary challenge Estonia faced was gaining public trust. Many Estonian citizens expressed concerns about the fairness and transparency of AI-made judicial decisions. While Estonia had a track record of successfully implementing digital innovations, the judiciary was seen as a domain where human judgment, empathy, and discretion were critical.

Public resistance stemmed from the fear that AI lacked the ability to account for the complexities and nuances of human interactions. A common argument was that AI, which is reliant on pre-programmed algorithms and data inputs, could not understand the context behind legal disputes. For example, in a landlord-tenant dispute, the underlying social and emotional factors might significantly affect the case, and critics argued that these nuances could be overlooked by an AI system.

2. Technological Limitations and Bias

Estonia's AI judiciary project also faced technological hurdles. AI systems rely heavily on past data, and training an AI to make judicial decisions requires feeding it historical case data. Estonia encountered problems with data quality and consistency. The AI was not always able to make well-informed decisions because it was working with incomplete or biased data, particularly in cases that dealt with marginalized communities.

There were fears that the AI might unintentionally perpetuate bias if it was trained on biased case law. For example, if historical judgments had consistently disadvantaged certain groups based on gender or socio-economic status, the AI could replicate these biases, leading to unjust decisions. This sparked a debate within the legal community about whether the AI should rely solely on past judgments or if there was a need to build in ethical guidelines to ensure fairness.

3. Resistance from Legal Professionals

Another key challenge was the resistance from judges, lawyers, and other legal professionals. Many judges expressed concerns that AI might undermine their role and authority. Estonia's judiciary had earned a reputation for fairness and efficiency, and the introduction of AI was seen as an encroachment on judicial independence.

Lawyers also voiced their opposition, particularly in small claims cases. They feared that the automated nature of AI judgments might lead to a "one-size-fits-all" approach, which could result in less personalized and thoughtful outcomes for clients. Additionally, the legal community was concerned about the lack of transparency in AI decision-making. Judges and lawyers were not able to fully understand the reasoning behind AI judgments, and without this transparency, they were unable to properly challenge or appeal rulings.

4. Ethical and Legal Framework

There was also the question of how to legally integrate AI into the judicial process. Estonia had to develop a clear legal framework to govern the use of AI in court, ensuring that the system complied with both Estonian law and EU regulations on data privacy, algorithmic accountability, and human rights. One concern was that AI rulings might not always align with constitutional principles, leading to legal challenges down the road.

Strategies for Overcoming Challenges

To address these challenges, Estonia adopted several key strategies:

1. Phased Implementation and Pilot Programs

Estonia initially limited the use of AI to small claims courts as part of a pilot program. By restricting AI to relatively low-stakes disputes, the government aimed to gather data and refine the system before expanding it to more complex cases. The pilot allowed Estonia to test the AI's capabilities and identify areas where human intervention might still be necessary.

Moreover, the AI system was designed to complement, rather than replace, human judges. If either party in a dispute disagreed with the AI's ruling, they had the option to appeal to a human judge. This gave people greater confidence in the system, knowing that human oversight remained a key component.

2. Public Awareness and Transparency

Estonia launched a public awareness campaign to explain how the AI system worked and to reassure citizens that human judges would still be involved in more complex or contentious cases. The government highlighted the benefits of using AI, such as faster case resolutions and reduced legal costs, while also emphasizing that the AI system would be regularly audited for fairness and bias.

To build transparency, Estonia's Ministry of Justice made efforts to explain how the AI made its decisions. Although AI is often seen as a "black box" technology, Estonia aimed to introduce transparency into the process by providing detailed reports on the AI's reasoning in individual cases. This helped demystify the technology and reduce concerns about arbitrary decisions.

3. Data Audits and Algorithmic Fairness

To address concerns about bias, Estonia implemented regular data audits to ensure that the AI was not making decisions based on discriminatory factors. The AI's training data was regularly updated to ensure that it reflected the evolving nature of legal cases and social attitudes. Estonia also worked with international experts to develop guidelines for algorithmic fairness, ensuring that the AI operated in accordance with EU human rights standards.

4. Involving Legal Professionals in the Development Process

To address resistance from judges and lawyers, Estonia actively involved legal professionals in the development and refinement of the AI system. The Ministry of Justice collaborated with judges and lawyers to ensure that the AI's design reflected the practical needs of the judiciary. This helped build trust among legal professionals, who appreciated having a say in how the system was developed.

The Estonian government also organized training programs to help legal professionals understand how to work alongside AI. These programs demonstrated how AI could assist with time-consuming tasks such as case document review, freeing up judges and lawyers to focus on more complex legal matters.

Successes Achieved

Despite the initial resistance and technological hurdles, Estonia achieved several successes with its AI judicial system.

1. Reduction in Case Backlogs

One of the most significant outcomes of the AI pilot was a noticeable reduction in the backlog of small claims cases. Previously, small claims cases could take months to resolve, but the AI system reduced resolution times to just a few weeks, and in some cases, days. This allowed the court to focus on more serious cases, improving overall efficiency.

2. Cost Savings for the Judiciary

The use of AI also led to cost savings for the Estonian judicial system. By automating small claims cases, the courts were able to reduce administrative expenses and lower the workload for court staff. As a result, the government could allocate more resources to more complex legal matters, further improving the quality of the judiciary's services.

3. Improved Access to Justice

Another benefit of Estonia's AI initiative was improved access to justice, particularly for individuals and businesses involved in small claims cases. The reduced legal costs and faster case resolutions made it easier for people to pursue legal claims, especially in disputes that might otherwise have been too costly or time-consuming to litigate.

4. Global Recognition and Influence

Estonia's success in integrating AI into its judicial system earned international recognition. Other countries, including Japan and South Korea, expressed interest in Estonia's AI judiciary model. Estonia's experiment also influenced discussions within the Eurpopean Union about the role of AI in legal systems, and the country became a leader in promoting ethical AI development within the judiciary.

Challenges That Persisted

1. Ongoing Ethical Concerns While Estonia made significant strides in addressing bias and transparency issues, there were still ethical concerns that persisted. Despite implementing regular audits, the "black box" nature of AI remained a challenge. Many legal professionals and human rights advocates continued to question whether an algorithm could ever fully account for the complexities of human disputes, especially when factors such as cultural, emotional, or social contexts came into play. Critics argued that the AI system could still unintentionally replicate biases found in past case data, particularly when handling cases involving marginalized or minority groups. Although Estonia's system allowed for human oversight, some feared that reliance on AI might reduce the perceived importance of judicial empathy and discretion.

2. Technological Maintenance and Updates As with any technology, Estonia faced ongoing challenges in maintaining and updating the AI system. The AI required regular data inputs, and the legal landscape was constantly evolving. New laws, changing social norms, and legal precedents had to be continually incorporated into the system to keep it relevant and accurate. Additionally, the system's developers had to stay on top of any issues that arose, such as bugs or incorrect rulings made by the AI. As Estonia expanded the AI's use, the need for constant updates and technological maintenance became a resource-intensive task.

3. Reluctance in Expanding Beyond Small Claims While AI proved to be effective in small claims courts, expanding its use to more complex legal matters encountered resistance. Judges, lawyers, and legal scholars were hesitant to introduce AI into areas of law that required more nuanced interpretation, such as family law, criminal cases, or constitutional matters. In such cases, the stakes were much higher, and there was widespread reluctance to entrust AI with decisions that could profoundly impact people's lives and freedoms. Estonia's initial plan to expand AI beyond small claims courts was put on hold as it became clear that the public and legal professionals were not ready to accept AI in these domains.

4. Lack of Public Understanding Despite public awareness campaigns, many Estonian citizens remained unsure about how AI worked within the judicial system. This lack of understanding fed into skepticism and mistrust. Although the Ministry of Justice provided transparency reports, explaining the AI's decision-making process was often complicated by the technical nature of the algorithms involved. Many people still feared that the system might make arbitrary decisions, and the complexity of AI technology created a barrier to full public acceptance.

Conclusion

Estonia's integration of AI into its judicial system marked a groundbreaking experiment in the application of technology to modernize the courts. By leveraging AI to handle small claims cases, Estonia successfully demonstrated that AI could improve judicial efficiency, reduce case backlogs, and lower legal costs. The system also provided improved access to justice for individuals and small businesses involved in minor disputes.

However, Estonia's experience also highlighted the challenges of introducing AI into a deeply human-centered domain like the judiciary. The country faced significant hurdles in building public trust, ensuring fairness and transparency, and addressing the ethical and technological challenges inherent in AI. While the pilot program showed promise, expanding AI into more complex legal areas remained a contentious issue, and the long-term success of AI in the judiciary depended on continuous oversight, adaptation, and careful implementation.

Estonia's experiment offers valuable lessons for other countries considering similar initiatives. It underscores the importance of transparency, human oversight, and public engagement in the development of AI-based legal systems. Moving forward, Estonia's pioneering efforts may serve as a blueprint for how to harness the power of AI in ways that enhance, rather than undermine, the fairness and integrity of judicial processes.

References

1. e-Estonia. "How Estonia Built a Digital Society: e-Governance and Beyond." Retrieved from e-estonia.com.

2. Latham & Watkins LLP. "The Rise of Artificial Intelligence in the Legal Profession: Implications and Challenges." *Law Review Journal*, 2020.

3. The Guardian. "Estonia's AI Judges: The Future of Justice?" February 2020. Retrieved from The Guardian.

4. Saar, Tanel. "AI and the Judiciary: Estonia's Experience." *Estonian Law Review*, 2021.

5. European Union Agency for Fundamental Rights (FRA). "AI and Algorithmic Accountability in Europe: Challenges and Legal Framework." *EU FRA Reports*, 2020. Retrieved from fra.europa.eu.

AI-Supported Legal Research in Complex Corporate Litigation

Introduction

In 2021, a prominent U.S.-based law firm, Briggs & Myers LLP, was tasked with defending a multinational corporation, FinTrust, in a complex corporate litigation case involving allegations of breach of fiduciary duty, financial fraud, and violation of securities law. The case was highly intricate, involving cross-border transactions, multiple subsidiaries, and complex financial arrangements spanning various jurisdictions.

As the firm prepared for litigation, it became clear that traditional legal research methods would be insufficient to handle the vast amount of legal precedents, statutes, and financial data required to build a robust defense. The team decided to incorporate AI-supported legal research tools, specifically ROSS Intelligence and CaseText, into their research strategy. These AI platforms provided enhanced capabilities for case law research, document review, and even predictive analysis.

This case study explores how AI-assisted legal research tools helped the legal team at Briggs & Myers LLP efficiently manage the immense workload, prepare for trial, and ultimately secure a favorable outcome for their client. It also highlights the challenges faced by the legal team, the ethical considerations of using AI, and the broader implications of AI adoption in legal practice.

Background: The Complexity of the Case

The case involved a class action lawsuit against FinTrust, a global investment firm accused of misleading investors by concealing the financial health of its international subsidiaries. The plaintiffs alleged that FinTrust's senior executives had failed to disclose crucial information about the deteriorating financial state of its European branch, leading to massive losses for investors when the subsidiary eventually declared bankruptcy.

Key legal issues in the case included:

1. **Cross-Border Financial Transactions:** The case involved multiple jurisdictions, requiring extensive research into both U.S. and European securities laws.

2. **Corporate Governance:** The plaintiffs claimed that FinTrust's executives had breached their fiduciary duties by withholding material information from investors and shareholders.

3. **Securities Law Violations:** The plaintiffs argued that FinTrust had violated the Securities Exchange Act by making false statements to investors regarding its financial condition.

The defense team at Briggs & Myers LLP faced the daunting task of sifting through decades of corporate filings, financial records, internal communications, and legal precedents from multiple jurisdictions. The traditional approach of using paralegals and junior associates for manual research would have been time-consuming and prone to error. With trial dates looming, the firm turned to AI-powered legal research tools to expedite the process.

AI Tools Deployed in the Case

1. ROSS Intelligence

ROSS Intelligence is an AI-powered legal research tool that uses natural language processing (NLP) to search and analyze case law. Unlike traditional keyword-based search engines, ROSS allows lawyers to ask legal questions in plain English and receive highly relevant results that are tailored to the specific legal issues at hand.

2. CaseText

CaseText is another AI-powered platform that provides advanced legal research capabilities. It uses a feature called "Parallel Search", which allows lawyers to find cases that are conceptually similar to the one they are researching, even if the exact legal terms or citations are not present. CaseText also offers document analysis tools that can review briefs, pleadings, and legal filings to suggest relevant cases or statutes that may have been overlooked.

By deploying these tools, the defence team was able to streamline several critical aspects of their case preparation, including legal research, document review, and case prediction analysis.

How AI Supported Legal Research in the Case

1. Efficient Case Law Search

One of the first tasks for the legal team was to identify relevant case law involving corporate governance and fiduciary duties. Traditionally, this would have required paralegals and junior associates to spend countless hours searching legal databases and reviewing case law manually. However, by using ROSS, the team was able to enter plain-language queries such as, "What are the fiduciary duties of executives in a multinational corporation?" and "Can executives be held liable for failing to disclose financial information about a subsidiary?"

Within minutes, ROSS returned a list of highly relevant case law, including Smith v. Van Gorkom (1985), a landmark U.S. Supreme Court case that established the legal precedent for the duty of care owed by corporate executives to shareholders. The AI platform also highlighted recent cases involving cross-border corporate transactions and fiduciary duty, saving the team weeks of manual research.

In addition to U.S. case law, the team used ROSS to search European legal databases for relevant precedents under EU corporate and securities law. The platform's NLP capabilities allowed the legal team to input complex, jurisdiction-specific questions, significantly reducing the time required to compile relevant case law from international courts.

2. Document Review and Analysis

The discovery phase of the case involved reviewing thousands of documents, including internal communications, corporate filings, and financial records from multiple subsidiaries. The sheer volume of documents presented a major challenge to the legal team, especially given the need to identify key pieces of evidence that could either support or undermine the plaintiff's allegations.

CaseText's CARA A.I., an AI-powered document review tool, proved invaluable during this phase. The CARA A.I. feature allowed the legal team to upload key legal documents—such as the complaint, briefs, and financial reports—and have the AI analyze the contents. Based on the uploaded documents, CaseText identified related cases, statutes, and legal principles that the team had not yet considered.

This was particularly useful when the legal team needed to build a defense around FinTrust's corporate governance structure. By uploading the company's bylaws and board meeting minutes, the AI identified legal principles from Delaware corporate law that emphasized the "business judgment rule"—a key doctrine that protects executives from personal liability when their decisions are made in good faith and with reasonable care. This discovery allowed the team to mount a stronger defense by arguing that the executives had acted within the scope of their fiduciary duties.

3. Predictive Legal Analytics

In addition to assisting with legal research and document review, AI tools like ROSS and CaseText provided predictive analytics that helped the legal team anticipate potential challenges in court. These tools analyzed the case law and historical rulings of the presiding judge to identify patterns in decision-making.

For example, by analyzing Judge Linda K. Murray's past rulings in securities cases, the AI tool predicted that she would be particularly concerned with issues of transparency and disclosure. This insight helped the defense team tailor their arguments to address the judge's likely concerns, focusing on how FinTrust had made substantial efforts to disclose financial information in good faith, even though some material information about its European subsidiary's financial troubles had been delayed.

4. Comparative Case Search with Parallel Search

Another major hurdle was finding analogous cases that involved similar cross-border financial fraud issues, particularly in the absence of identical legal terms or citations. This is where CaseText's Parallel Search proved critical. The AI engine found conceptually similar cases across different legal systems, allowing the team to identify case law from other jurisdictions that had similar fact patterns but did not share exact legal terminology.

For example, the legal team was able to uncover a key European Court of Justice ruling from 2018 that addressed the disclosure obligations of multinational corporations with complex subsidiary structures. While the case did not cite the same statutes or legal principles as U.S. law, the AI identified a conceptual similarity in how the court approached fiduciary duties and financial disclosures, which ultimately helped the team strengthen its defense strategy.

Challenges and Ethical Considerations

While the use of AI tools significantly enhanced the legal team's efficiency and ability to handle the case's complexities, it also raised several challenges and ethical considerations.

1. Over-Reliance on AI

One concern voiced by some members of the legal team was the potential for over-reliance on AI-generated results. AI tools are only as effective as the data they are trained on, and there was a fear that relying too heavily on AI suggestions might cause the team to overlook important nuances that only human judgment could catch. To mitigate this, the team used AI as a supplementary tool, ensuring that human attorneys still reviewed and analyzed all findings generated by the AI.

2. Bias in Training Data

Another ethical concern related to the potential for bias in the AI's training data. If the AI tools had been trained primarily on past case law that reflected historical biases (e.g., judgments that disproportionately favored large corporations over small investors), there was a risk that the AI could reinforce those biases in its recommendations. This issue was particularly relevant given the plaintiffs' accusations that FinTrust had exploited small, vulnerable investors. To address this, the legal team cross-referenced AI results with broader legal sources to ensure that their arguments were balanced and free of bias.

3. Confidentiality and Data Security

Given the sensitive nature of the documents being processed—many of which contained confidential financial information—data security was a significant concern. The legal team worked closely with the AI tool providers to ensure that all data was encrypted and stored securely, preventing any breaches or unauthorized access.

Outcome of the Case

Thanks to the efficiency and accuracy provided by AI-supported legal research tools, the legal team at Briggs & Myers LLP was able to build a comprehensive defense strategy that addressed the complex legal issues surrounding fiduciary duty, corporate governance, and securities law. During the trial, the defense successfully argued that FinTrust's executives had acted in good faith and had made reasonable efforts to disclose the financial difficulties of their European subsidiary.

The use of AI tools not only expedited the research process but also allowed the team to uncover key legal principles and precedents that may have otherwise been missed. In the end, the court ruled in favor of FinTrust, dismissing the most serious claims of fraud and breach of fiduciary duty. While the company was required to pay a modest settlement to the plaintiffs, it avoided significant financial penalties andwas able to prevent any reputational damage from impacting its global operations.

Broader Implications for AI in Legal Practice

This case highlights several important implications for the legal profession as it increasingly adopts AI tools:

1. **Enhanced Efficiency and Accuracy:** AI-supported legal research tools like ROSS Intelligence and CaseText enable law firms to handle vast amounts of data more efficiently, reducing research time and improving accuracy. In complex cases, particularly those involving cross-border issues, AI can process and synthesize information at a scale that would be impossible for human researchers alone.

2. **Human-AI Collaboration:** The case also demonstrates that AI tools are most effective when used in collaboration with human legal professionals. While AI can assist in identifying relevant legal principles and precedents, human judgment remains critical in interpreting results and applying them to specific cases.

3. **Ethical Considerations and Transparency:** The use of AI in legal research raises important ethical questions about bias, over-reliance, and transparency. Law firms must take steps to ensure that AI tools are used responsibly, avoiding the potential for bias in decision-making and maintaining client confidentiality.

4. **AI Adoption in the Legal Industry:** The success of AI in this case may encourage further adoption of AI tools across the legal profession. As more law firms begin to integrate AI into their practices, it is likely that AI will play an increasingly important role in legal research, litigation, and even case prediction.

Conclusion

The use of AI-supported legal research tools in the FinTrust corporate litigation case illustrates how AI can significantly enhance a law firm's ability to manage complex cases. By automating time-consuming tasks such as case law search and document review, AI tools allowed the defense team at Briggs & Myers LLP to focus on developing a robust legal strategy, ultimately securing a favorable outcome for their client.

However, the case also highlights the need for caution. As AI becomes more prevalent in the legal profession, law firms must remain mindful of the ethical considerations and limitations of AI systems. Human oversight, transparency, and a balanced approach are essential to ensuring that AI serves as a valuable tool for lawyers without compromising fairness or accuracy in legal proceedings.

References

1. ROSS Intelligence. (2021). "How AI is Transforming Legal Research." Retrieved from rossintelligence.com

2. CaseText. (2021). "Harnessing the Power of AI in Legal Research." Retrieved from casetext.com

3. McGinnis, J.O., & Pearce, R.G. (2014). "The Great Disruption: How Machine Intelligence Will Transform the Role of Lawyers in the Delivery of Legal Services." *Fordham Law Review*, 82(6), 3041-3066.

4. Silver, C. (2021). "AI and Legal Ethics: Navigating the New Frontiers of Artificial Intelligence in Legal Practice." *ABA Journal*. Retrieved from abajournal.com

5. Surden, H. (2020). "Artificial Intelligence and Law: An Overview." *American Law Review*.

AI Failure in the U.S. Criminal Justice System – The Controversy of COMPAS

Introduction

In 2016, an investigative report by ProPublica brought the controversial use of AI-based risk assessment tools in the U.S. criminal justice system to the forefront. The focus of the report was COMPAS (Correctional Offender Management Profiling for Alternative Sanctions), an AI-powered tool designed to predict the likelihood of a defendant reoffending. COMPAS was developed by Northpointe (now Equivant) and had been adopted by numerous states across the U.S. to assist judges in making pre-trial bail decisions, sentencing, and parole determinations.

COMPAS was seen as a revolutionary tool that could reduce biases and improve efficiency in the justice system by providing data-driven assessments of an offender's risk level. However, the tool became the center of a heated debate when the ProPublica investigation revealed that COMPAS was systematically biased against African American defendants, assigning them higher risk scores compared to white defendants with similar criminal histories. This case study explores the background, deployment, and subsequent controversy surrounding COMPAS, examining how the AI tool failed in its promise to create a more just and equitable system and sparked widespread discussions about AI ethics in the legal domain.

Background: The Role of COMPAS in the Criminal Justice System

COMPAS was introduced to the criminal justice system as a means to improve judicial decision-making by offering a statistical analysis of a defendant's likelihood of reoffending, known as recidivism. By analyzing data such as criminal history, demographic information, employment status, and social factors, COMPAS produced a risk score intended to assist judges in determining whether to grant bail, impose harsher sentences, or approve parole.

The rationale behind adopting COMPAS and other similar tools was twofold:

1. **Reducing Subjective Bias:** The U.S. criminal justice system has long struggled with racial disparities in sentencing and bail decisions. Proponents of COMPAS argued that by relying on objective data, the tool could reduce human biases and help create fairer judicial outcomes.

2. **Improving Efficiency:** Courts are notoriously overburdened, with judges and parole officers facing heavy caseloads. COMPAS was designed to streamline the decision-making process by providing judges with a quick and reliable assessment of each defendant's risk, allowing courts to function more efficiently.

How COMPAS Works

COMPAS uses a proprietary algorithm that assesses over 100 factors related to an offender's background, including:

- **Criminal history:** Number of previous arrests and convictions.

- **Demographics:** Age, gender, and sometimes race.

- **Social and economic factors:** Employment status, educational attainment, and neighborhood.

- **Psychological factors:** Answers to questions about criminal attitudes and behaviors, which are part of a questionnaire that defendants fill out during pre-trial assessments.

Based on these inputs, COMPAS generates risk scores in several categories, most notably the likelihood of general recidivism and violent recidivism. These risk scores are then provided to judges to inform their decisions about bail, sentencing, or parole.

The Controversy: ProPublica's Investigation

In May 2016, ProPublica released a detailed investigative report that examined the risk scores generated by COMPAS in Broward County, Florida. The investigation focused on over 7,000 defendants and analyzed their COMPAS risk scores alongside their actual rates of recidivism over a two-year period. The results revealed a disturbing pattern of racial bias:

- Black defendants were more likely to be labeled as "high risk" for reoffending, even though they did not reoffend at higher rates than white defendants.

- Conversely, white defendants were often labeled as "low risk" but were found to reoffend at similar or higher rates compared to their black counterparts.

For example, the report highlighted the cases of Vernon Prater and Brisha Borden:

- Brisha Borden, a young African American woman, received a high COMPAS risk score despite being arrested for a minor incident (attempting to steal a bicycle). She was rated as high-risk despite no serious prior offenses, and yet she did not commit another crime during the observation period.

- Vernon Prater, a white man with a lengthy criminal history, was rated low-risk, yet he went on to commit further crimes after his release. This stark contrast between the risk assessments and actual outcomes was one of the core examples of how COMPAS's algorithm was flawed and racially biased.

Algorithmic Bias: Understanding the Root Cause

The main issue with COMPAS lay in the training data used to develop the algorithm and the factors that were considered in its decision-making process. While the system itself did not explicitly consider race as a factor, many of the inputs used to generate risk scores, such as criminal history and socioeconomic data, were correlated with race due to systemic inequalities in policing, economic opportunities, and social structures.

For instance, African Americans are disproportionately more likely to be arrested for minor offenses due to over-policing in their communities. This historical pattern of racial disparity in law enforcement created biased data that fed into the COMPAS system. As a result, the AI tool perpetuated and exacerbated the very biases it was supposed to reduce.

Additionally, because COMPAS is a proprietary system, the algorithm's inner workings were not transparent. This lack of transparency made it impossible for defendants and legal professionals to challenge or understand the factors that led to their high-risk assessments. Judges, too, were often unable to fully grasp how COMPAS had arrived at its conclusions, making them more likely to rely on its risk assessments without questioning their validity.

Legal and Ethical Implications

The ProPublica investigation ignited a broader debate about the ethical implications of using AI in judicial decision-making. Several key concerns were raised:

1. **Due Process Concerns:** The lack of transparency in COMPAS's algorithm led to concerns about defendants' rights to a fair trial. The U.S. Constitution guarantees individuals the right to challenge the evidence used against them, but because COMPAS's algorithm was proprietary and opaque, defendants were often unable to challenge their risk assessments. This raised significant questions about whether the use of AI in courtrooms violated the principles of due process.

2. **Reinforcement of Racial Disparities:** Instead of reducing racial disparities in the criminal justice system, COMPAS appeared to

reinforce them. By disproportionately labeling African Americans as high-risk, the tool contributed to harsher sentencing and bail conditions for black defendants. This further entrenched the systemic racial inequalities that already existed in the criminal justice system.

3. **Judicial Over-Reliance on AI:** Judges using COMPAS were often unaware of the algorithm's limitations. Many judges may have over-relied on the AI's risk assessments without fully considering the broader context of each defendant's circumstances. This led to concerns that judges were abdicating their responsibility to exercise human judgment and discretion in favor of algorithmic decisions.

The Aftermath: Calls for Reform and Policy Responses

The revelations from the ProPublica investigation prompted immediate calls for reform. Civil rights organizations, including the ACLU and Electronic Frontier Foundation, demanded greater transparency and accountability for AI systems used in the legal system. The debate extended beyond COMPAS to other risk assessment tools, sparking a wider conversation about the role of AI in criminal justice.

In response to the controversy, several states began reconsidering their use of COMPAS and similar tools. Some jurisdictions initiated independent audits of their AI-based risk assessment systems to identify and mitigate biases. Others began exploring alternative approaches, such as using open-source algorithms that could be reviewed and scrutinized by the public.

Additionally, some legal scholars and policymakers called for "algorithmic accountability" laws, which would require companies that develop AI systems for the public sector to disclose their algorithms and make them open to third-party audits. These laws would aim to ensure that AI systems are transparent, fair, and accountable to the people they impact.

Ongoing Debate: The Future of AI in Criminal Justice

Despite the controversy surrounding COMPAS, the debate about AI in criminal justice is far from settled. While the flaws in COMPAS have been well-documented, many proponents argue that AI tools still hold great promise for improving the fairness and efficiency of the legal system—if they are designed and implemented responsibly.

One proposed solution to the bias problem is to develop "fairness-aware" algorithms, which would explicitly account for potential biases in the data and adjust their calculations accordingly. These algorithms could be designed to minimize disparities in risk scores between different demographic groups, ensuring that AI systems do not exacerbate existing inequalities.

At the same time, there are ongoing discussions about the need for more rigorous testing and validation of AI systems before they are deployed in the legal system. Some experts advocate for AI to be used as a complement to human judgment, rather than a replacement. Under this model, AI tools would provide judges with additional insights, but the ultimate decision-making power would remain with human judges who are better equipped to understand the nuances of individual cases.

Conclusion

The case of COMPAS represents a pivotal moment in the intersection of AI and criminal justice. While AI risk assessment tools were introduced with the promise of reducing bias and improving judicial decision-making, the experience with COMPAS highlights the dangers of relying too heavily on flawed algorithms without sufficient oversight or transparency. The case underscores the need for careful consideration of the ethical implications of AI and the importance of developing fair, transparent, and accountable systems that can truly deliver on their promises.

The controversy surrounding COMPAS has sparked an important conversation about the role of AI in the justice system, one that will continue to shape the future of AI adoption in courts around the world.

References

1. ProPublica - Julia Angwin, Jeff Larson, Surya Mattu, and Lauren Kirchner. *Machine Bias: There's Software Used Across the Country to Predict Future Criminals. And It's Biased Against Blacks.* ProPublica, May 23, 2016. Retrieved from: ProPublica

2. Equivant (formerly Northpointe) - "COMPAS Risk & Needs Assessment."

    Equivant's official site provides details about the COMPAS tool and how it is used in criminal justice systems. Retrieved from: Equivant

3. The Guardian - "The Racist Algorithm: How Risk Assessment Tools Disproportionately Affect African Americans."

    This article explains how algorithms like COMPAS have been criticized for reinforcing racial biases in the U.S. legal system. Retrieved from: The Guardian

4. Harvard Law Review - "Algorithmic Risk Assessments and the Legal System."

    A detailed analysis of the legal and ethical concerns regarding algorithmic risk assessment tools, focusing on the COMPAS controversy. Retrieved from: Harvard Law Review

5. Electronic Frontier Foundation (EFF) - "Artificial Intelligence and Racial Bias in Risk Assessment Tools."

    EFF has explored the impact of AI tools like COMPAS on civil liberties and racial bias in criminal justice. Retrieved from: EFF

6. American Civil Liberties Union (ACLU) - "Risk Assessments in Criminal Justice: What We Know and What We Don't."

    The ACLU provides an overview of risk assessment tools like COMPAS and their implications for racial equity in sentencing. Retrieved from: ACLU

AI-Assisted Legal Process in Small Claims Court – A Citizen's Journey to Justice

Introduction

In 2023, Sarah Thompson, a small business owner from California, found herself in a legal dispute with a supplier who failed to deliver essential equipment for her catering business. The delay caused significant financial losses as Sarah was unable to meet several client deadlines. With no resolution in sight after multiple failed negotiations, Sarah decided to pursue the matter through small claims court. However, unfamiliar with legal processes and wary of the costs of hiring a lawyer, Sarah turned to a recently launched AI-powered platform designed to assist citizens like her in navigating the legal system.

This case study follows Sarah's journey, from filing her case to its resolution, focusing on how AI-supported tools transformed her experience by providing transparency, efficiency, and access to justice.

Background: The Dispute

Sarah's dispute arose from a contract she had signed with WestCo Supply, a company that specialized in delivering kitchen equipment to small businesses. Under the terms of their agreement, WestCo was supposed to deliver $8,000 worth of appliances within 30 days. However, the company repeatedly delayed the shipment without adequate explanation, leaving Sarah with no choice but to rent substitute equipment at additional costs.

After several unsuccessful attempts to negotiate a refund or faster delivery, Sarah estimated that her financial losses amounted to nearly $12,000, including lost business opportunities, rental fees, and damaged client relationships. Unsure of her legal rights and unable to afford an attorney, Sarah initially felt powerless. But after researching online, she discovered a new AI-driven platform, JusticeTech, designed to help small business owners and citizens navigate legal disputes without the need for costly legal representation.

JusticeTech: The AI Platform

JusticeTech was developed as part of a broader initiative in California to improve access to justice in small claims courts, particularly for individuals and small business owners unfamiliar with legal procedures. The platform combined several AI tools to assist with:

1. **Case Filing and Preparation:** AI guided users through the process of drafting a claim, ensuring that all necessary information was included.

2. **Legal Document Generation:** The platform provided templates for demand letters, case summaries, and court filings, which were customized based on user inputs.

3. **Case Law Search and Analysis:** AI offered suggestions on similar cases and relevant statutes to help users better understand the legal context of their dispute.

4. **Settlement Negotiations:** AI-powered mediation tools helped facilitate settlement talks between the parties before the case went to trial.

5. **Court Simulation:** The platform also simulated courtroom scenarios, allowing users to prepare for their appearance before a judge.

Filing the Case with AI Support

Once Sarah decided to file her case, she registered with JusticeTech. The platform guided her step by step through the filing process. The AI interface asked Sarah a series of questions:

- What was the nature of the dispute?
- How much financial damage had the breach of contract caused?
- Had she attempted to negotiate a settlement with the supplier?
- Did she have any documents (such as emails or receipts) to support her claims?

Based on her answers, the AI generated a draft of her small claims complaint, automatically populating the relevant sections with information from Sarah's responses. Sarah was also able to upload the emails between her and WestCo, which the AI scanned for key details like the dates of communication, promised delivery times, and the supplier's failure to meet deadlines.

Within an hour, Sarah had a fully drafted small claims court filing, ready to be submitted to the court. The AI also generated a summary of California contract law, highlighting sections that were relevant to her case, such as the state's laws on breach of contract and failure to deliver goods as promised.

Pre-Trial: AI-Assisted Mediation and Settlement Negotiation

Before Sarah's case went to trial, JusticeTech's AI offered to facilitate a mediation process between her and WestCo. The platform's AI analyzed the case details, financial records, and similar past cases and suggested potential settlement amounts that might be acceptable to both parties.

The AI recommended a $10,000 settlement based on its assessment of Sarah's financial losses and the likelihood that she would win in court. JusticeTech then sent a formal settlement offer to WestCo's legal team on Sarah's behalf.

Initially, WestCo countered with a low offer of $6,000. However, with the AI's continued mediation and analysis of past case outcomes, the platform proposed a new middle ground, offering a $9,000 settlement as a compromise. After several rounds of negotiation, both parties eventually agreed to settle for $9,500.

For Sarah, this AI-assisted mediation process saved both time and the potential stress of a court appearance, all while avoiding the costs associated with hiring a lawyer. In this case, the use of AI in settlement negotiations not only provided an efficient resolution but also gave Sarah a better understanding of what a fair settlement might look like, which boosted her confidence during the negotiation process.

Transparency and Legal Education

One of the most significant benefits Sarah experienced from JusticeTech was the transparency and education the platform provided. Traditionally, small claims court processes can be opaque for those without legal expertise. However, the AI's real-time explanations and contextual links to legal statutes made it easier for Sarah to understand the law and how it applied to her case.

For example, when Sarah asked about the possibility of WestCo counter-suing her, the AI provided a simple, jargon-free explanation of California's counterclaim laws and clarified the circumstances under which WestCo might have a legal basis for doing so. This helped Sarah feel more in control of her legal situation and alleviated her fears of unforeseen consequences.

JusticeTech also provided Sarah with a courtroom simulation feature, which walked her through what to expect during a court appearance, including sample questions a judge might ask and tips on how to present her evidence effectively. Though her case was resolved through settlement, Sarah appreciated this preparation, as it gave her confidence that she could handle a trial if necessary.

The Outcome and Resolution

Sarah's case never reached the courtroom. Thanks to the AI-powered mediation tools, Sarah and WestCo reached a satisfactory settlement of $9,500. The settlement covered Sarah's financial losses, including the cost of rental equipment, lost business opportunities, and damages to her business reputation.

The use of JusticeTech allowed Sarah to resolve her legal dispute without ever hiring a lawyer, which saved her thousands of dollars in legal fees. It also helped her avoid the emotional strain and uncertainty of a court trial, as the AI mediation system facilitated productive negotiations between both parties.

Moreover, JusticeTech provided Sarah with an invaluable education about her legal rights and the court process, making her feel more empowered and better informed throughout the process.

Challenges and Ethical Considerations

While Sarah's experience with AI in the legal process was largely positive, there are broader ethical and technical considerations to consider when using AI tools in civil disputes:

1. **Data Privacy:** Uploading sensitive business information (such as contracts and financial records) to an AI platform raises concerns about data security. Sarah was initially hesitant to trust an online system with her private documents, though JusticeTech assured her that all data was encrypted.

2. **Algorithmic Decision-Making:** AI mediation tools rely on historical data to recommend settlements. There is a risk that such tools could reinforce existing biases, especially if past cases reflect unequal outcomes for certain demographics or business sectors. In Sarah's case, the AI suggested a fair settlement based on the specifics of her dispute, but this may not always be the case for other users.

3. **Lack of Human Oversight:** While AI can provide fast and affordable legal assistance, it does not replace the nuanced understanding of a human lawyer. There was a concern that had Sarah's case been more complex, the AI might not have been able to fully capture the intricacies of her legal arguments. This raises questions about the limits of AI in more complicated or emotionally charged cases.

4. **Digital Divide:** While platforms like JusticeTech improve access to justice for tech-savvy individuals, they may unintentionally exclude citizens who lack access to technology or are unfamiliar with using digital tools. Efforts must be made to ensure that AI-driven legal services are inclusive and accessible to all segments of society.

Conclusion

Sarah Thompson's case demonstrates how AI-powered legal platforms like JusticeTech can transform the small claims court process for citizens and small business owners, making justice more accessible, transparent, and affordable. By providing AI-driven tools for case preparation, mediation, and legal education, JusticeTech allowed Sarah to resolve her dispute efficiently and equitably without the need for costly legal representation.

However, this case also highlights the importance of ensuring that AI systems are used responsibly, with adequate protections for data privacy, fairness, and inclusivity. As AI continues to play a larger role in the legal process, its developers and regulators must carefully consider the ethical implications of relying on algorithmic decision-making in matters of justice.

References

1. ProPublica. "How AI is Transforming Legal Processes for Small Claims Courts." Retrieved from: ProPublica

2. Harvard Law Review. "Artificial Intelligence and Access to Justice: Opportunities and Risks in Civil Disputes." Retrieved from: Harvard Law Review

3. California Courts. "The Impact of AI on Access to Justice in Small Claims Courts." Retrieved from: California Courts

4. JusticeTech. "How AI Mediation Can Help Resolve Legal Disputes." Retrieved from: JusticeTech

AI Integration in Criminal vs. Civil Law

Introduction

Artificial intelligence (AI) is transforming both criminal and civil law in distinct ways. In criminal law, AI is used primarily for risk assessments, sentencing, and bail decisions, while in civil law, AI plays a role in dispute resolution, contract analysis, and out-of-court settlements. This case study contrasts AI's application in both domains, examining how AI tools are reshaping judicial outcomes and addressing different ethical concerns in criminal versus civil proceedings.

Case Study A: AI in Criminal Law – Sentencing and Risk Assessment

Background

In 2020, John Miller, a 35-year-old individual with a criminal history of non-violent offenses, was arrested for drug possession and burglary in Chicago, Illinois. Given his prior convictions, the court used COMPAS (Correctional Offender Management Profiling for Alternative Sanctions), an AI-based risk assessment tool, to determine whether Miller posed a high risk of reoffending. The results of the COMPAS assessment would influence the judge's decision regarding pre-trial bail and the eventual sentencing.

COMPAS was designed to assess various factors such as criminal history, socioeconomic background, and responses to behavioral questionnaires. Based on these inputs, the tool generates a recidivism score that categorizes defendants into low, medium, or high risk of reoffending.

The AI's Role in Decision-Making

1. Bail Decision After his arrest, the COMPAS system assessed Miller as a medium risk for general recidivism but a high risk for violent recidivism. Based on this assessment, the judge set a higher bail than might have been expected for a non-violent crime, concerned that Miller could potentially escalate into more serious criminal behavior. The AI recommendation played a significant role in the judge's decision, although the final decision was made by the judge.

2. Sentencing Upon conviction, COMPAS also influenced Miller's sentencing. The AI system recommended a stricter sentence based on his risk profile and past criminal behavior. In addition to the standard jail time for the offenses, Miller was ordered to undergo drug rehabilitation and regular probation check-ins. The judge's decision reflected the AI's recommendation, relying on its data to justify a combination of punishment and rehabilitation, aiming to reduce the likelihood of recidivism.

Ethical Concerns in Criminal Law

The use of AI in Miller's case brings several ethical concerns to the forefront:

1. Bias in AI Models Despite COMPAS not directly considering race as a factor, studies have shown that the system can replicate historical racial biases found in the criminal justice system. Miller's demographic and social factors could have unduly influenced his high recidivism score, leading to harsher bail and sentencing conditions than warranted by his actual behavior.

   Example: A 2016 ProPublica investigation revealed that COMPAS disproportionately flagged African American defendants as high-risk compared to their white counterparts, even when controlling for similar criminal backgrounds.

2. Lack of Transparency COMPAS operates on a proprietary algorithm, meaning that defendants and their attorneys have little insight into how the AI arrives at its risk scores. In Miller's case, his lawyer could not challenge the AI's conclusions because the algorithm was not fully transparent. This lack of clarity raises due process concerns, as defendants may be unable to contest the factors that influence judicial decisions.

3. Over-reliance on AI Although COMPAS is designed to assist judges, there is a growing concern that judicial discretion is being overly influenced by AI recommendations. In Miller's case, the judge relied heavily on the risk assessment, possibly reducing the emphasis on a more individualized understanding of his circumstances.

Outcome and Discussion

John Miller's case underscores the dual-edged nature of AI in criminal law. While AI can help courts manage large caseloads efficiently and provide data-driven insights, it also raises concerns about fairness, bias, and the erosion of human judgment. The risk of AI perpetuating existing systemic biases, particularly racial disparities, must be addressed through more transparent and accountable algorithms.

Case Study B: AI in Civil Law – Out-of-Court Settlements

Background

In 2022, Mary Johnson, a small business owner in New York, found herself in a contractual dispute with a supplier, TechParts Ltd., over defective electronic components delivered for her retail operation. Mary faced financial losses due to delays in product replacements, and after failing to negotiate directly with TechParts, she considered pursuing legal action in civil court.

Instead of going to court, Mary opted to use an AI-powered mediation tool called SmartMediation, which was designed to facilitate dispute resolution in small civil matters, including business-to-business (B2B) disputes. The AI platform provided both parties with legal guidance and suggested settlement amounts based on similar cases.

The AI's Role in Mediation

1. Legal Document Analysis and Case Suggestion SmartMediation began by analyzing the contract between Mary and TechParts, identifying clauses related to product quality and delivery times. The AI flagged a breach of contract and, using case law data, presented Mary with an overview of her legal options. Based on its analysis of similar cases, the system recommended a potential settlement figure of $20,000, covering her financial losses and additional damages.

2. Negotiation and Settlement TechParts initially countered with a lower settlement offer, but SmartMediation used AI-driven negotiation tactics to suggest a midpoint of $17,000. The AI analyzed both parties' financial positions and historical data on similar contract disputes to determine a fair settlement. After several rounds of AI-facilitated negotiations, both parties agreed to the $17,000 settlement, avoiding the need for a costly and lengthy trial.

Ethical Considerations in Civil Law

While AI integration in civil law provides clear benefits, especially in terms of efficiency and accessibility, it also raises ethical and procedural concerns:

1. Efficiency vs. Human Understanding AI tools like SmartMediation can process contracts and legal documents faster than humans, offering quick and cost-effective dispute resolution. However, critics argue that AI lacks the human intuition necessary for understanding the emotional and relational aspects of civil disputes, particularly in family law or cases involving personal injury.

   Example: In contract disputes like Mary's, AI may effectively calculate fair compensation based on precedent, but in family law cases involving child custody or alimony, human judges are better suited to consider the emotional nuances that AI cannot quantify.

2. Data Privacy For AI to perform accurate analyses, parties in civil disputes must upload sensitive business contracts and financial records to the platform. While platforms like SmartMediation encrypt data for security, there is always a risk of data breaches or misuse of sensitive information, which raises concerns about privacy.

3. Algorithmic Fairness AI in civil disputes relies heavily on past case data. If prior legal decisions are biased or flawed, AI tools could perpetuate these problems by basing new recommendations on biased outcomes. Although less impactful than in criminal law, this issue still raises concerns about fairness in civil cases.

Outcome and Discussion

Mary's case highlights the advantages of AI in civil law: efficiency, cost savings, and quicker access to justice. For small business owners like Mary, AI tools offer a practical alternative to expensive litigation, allowing disputes to be resolved through objective data and past legal precedent. However, these systems must be carefully designed to ensure fairness and transparency, particularly when the stakes involve personal or business relationships.

Conclusion

The integration of AI into both criminal and civil law brings significant benefits but also distinct ethical challenges. In criminal law, the use of AI in sentencing and risk assessment raises concerns about fairness, transparency, and the reinforcement of systemic biases. In contrast, AI in civil law is largely focused on efficiency and accessibility, facilitating quicker dispute resolution and mediation. However, it too faces issues related to algorithmic fairness and data privacy.

As AI continues to evolve within the legal system, it is critical that courts and policymakers establish clear guidelines for its use, ensuring that AI enhances rather than undermines justice in both criminal and civil contexts.

References

1. ProPublica. "Machine Bias: There's Software Used Across the Country to Predict Future Criminals. And It's Biased Against Blacks." Retrieved from ProPublica

2. Harvard Law Review. "Algorithmic Risk Assessments in Criminal Justice." Retrieved from Harvard Law Review

3. Equivant. "COMPAS Risk & Needs Assessment." Retrieved from Equivant

4. ABA Journal. "Artificial Intelligence and Its Impact on Civil Litigation." Retrieved from ABA Journal

5. SmartMediation. "AI Mediation and the Future of Dispute Resolution." Retrieved from SmartMediation

AI's Role in Resolving a Cross-Border Trade Dispute

Introduction

In 2022, two multinational companies, TechWorks Inc., based in the United States, and InfiniTech Ltd., based in Germany, became embroiled in a cross-border trade dispute over the non-fulfillment of a technology transfer agreement. The contract, worth approximately $50 million, stipulated that TechWorks would provide proprietary software and training services to InfiniTech for their use in an advanced manufacturing process. However, disputes arose over the quality of the software and the delays in providing the agreed services, leading to accusations of breach of contract by both parties.

Given the complexity of the case—spanning multiple jurisdictions, involving both U.S. and EU trade laws, and requiring nuanced understanding of intellectual property (IP) regulations—both parties agreed to resolve the dispute through international arbitration. To streamline the arbitration process, ArbitrAI, an AI-powered platform designed for cross-border arbitration, was employed. ArbitrAI analyzed the legal frameworks in both countries, recommended potential resolutions based on prior case law, and assisted in drafting settlement terms.

This case study explores how AI tools, like ArbitrAI, are increasingly being used in international arbitration to handle the complexities of multi-jurisdictional disputes. It also highlights how AI adapts to different national legal frameworks and addresses the challenges that arise in such cases.

Background: The Trade Dispute

The contract between TechWorks and InfiniTech was signed in 2021, and both companies expected the agreement to revolutionize InfiniTech's manufacturing processes. However, by mid-2022, InfiniTech filed a formal complaint, accusing TechWorks of delivering subpar software that did not meet the agreed specifications. InfiniTech also claimed that the delays in providing training services had caused substantial financial losses.

In response, TechWorks countered that InfiniTech had failed to follow the implementation guidelines correctly, and that the issues were due to improper use of the software rather than any flaw in the product itself. TechWorks demanded full payment for services rendered, while InfiniTech refused to pay until the problems were resolved. With both parties standing their ground, they turned to international arbitration under the auspices of the International Chamber of Commerce (ICC).

AI's Role in International Arbitration

1. Legal Analysis Across Jurisdictions

One of the first tasks ArbitrAI undertook was to perform a comprehensive analysis of the relevant laws in both the U.S. and Germany. Trade disputes of this nature typically involve complex regulations related to intellectual property, commercial contracts, and cross-border trade practices. ArbitrAI was fed the entire contract and documentation provided by both parties, allowing the AI system to compare the contractual obligations with relevant laws from both jurisdictions.

The AI system also analyzed relevant prior cases from both the U.S. and Germany, including similar disputes involving software delivery and IP rights. For example, in Germany, the German Commercial Code (HGB) and EU directives on software delivery were considered, while in the U.S., Uniform Commercial Code (UCC) provisions on contract performance and remedies were highlighted. By comparing these frameworks, ArbitrAI was able to suggest which laws would have precedence depending on the interpretation of various clauses in the contract.

2. Identifying Key Issues and Breach of Contract

The AI system identified several key areas of contention based on both the contract and the legal analysis. ArbitrAI flagged potential breaches of contract on both sides:

- **TechWorks:** Possible breach related to delivering a software product that did not meet the agreed-upon functionality standards.

- **InfiniTech:** Potential breach for refusing payment based on delays that were, according to TechWorks, a result of improper software use.

The AI also highlighted that both the U.S. and German legal systems allow for certain remedies in case of partial contract performance, such as adjusting the payment terms to reflect the value of services actually rendered.

3. Recommendation of Settlement Terms

Once the key issues were identified, ArbitrAI leveraged its database of similar cases and legal precedents to recommend potential settlement terms. The AI analyzed outcomes from over 100 similar cases involving cross-border trade disputes in the tech sector, providing a range of potential resolutions:

- **Partial Payment:** One suggestion involved InfiniTech making a partial payment of 60% of the contract value, contingent on TechWorks correcting the software issues and providing the required training.

- **Escrow Arrangement:** Another proposal was to set up an escrow account, where InfiniTech would deposit the remaining funds, to be released once the software met agreed-upon specifications.

- **Joint Expert Review:** ArbitrAI also recommended involving a third-party software expert to verify whether the software truly met the agreed-upon technical standards. This independent review would help resolve the technical dispute more objectively.

4. Predictive Analysis of Arbitration Outcome

ArbitrAI's predictive algorithms provided both parties with an analysis of the likely outcomes should the case proceed to formal arbitration. Based on past rulings in similar cases, the AI predicted that an arbitrator would likely favor a settlement rather than a complete victory for either party. Specifically, it estimated a 70% probability that InfiniTech would be required to make partial payments, with TechWorks obliged to address software issues and complete training.

By offering these predictive insights, ArbitrAI encouraged both parties to negotiate a settlement, saving time and costs associated with prolonged arbitration.

5. Drafting Settlement Agreement

Once both parties agreed to pursue a settlement based on ArbitrAI's recommendations, the platform's natural language processing (NLP) capabilities were used to draft a legally sound settlement agreement. The AI system incorporated the agreed terms, including partial payment, the establishment of an escrow account, and timelines for completing software fixes and training.

The AI-drafted document was reviewed by legal counsel on both sides to ensure compliance with both U.S. and EU legal standards. This reduced the time typically spent drafting and negotiating settlement terms manually, streamlining the arbitration process.

Complexities of Handling International Legal Frameworks

One of the most significant challenges in cross-border arbitration is navigating the different legal frameworks that govern contracts, trade practices, and intellectual property in different countries. In this case, ArbitrAI had to adapt to both U.S. and German laws, which differ in several key ways:

1. Contract Law Differences:

In the U.S., contracts are generally governed by the Uniform Commercial Code (UCC), which provides flexibility in terms of contract performance and remedies. In contrast, German law, governed by the German Commercial Code (HGB), places stricter requirements on the quality and timely delivery of goods. ArbitrAI accounted for these differences in its recommendations, balancing the U.S.'s more lenient approach with Germany's stricter legal provisions on commercial contracts.

2. Intellectual Property Regulations:

Intellectual property law varies significantly between jurisdictions. ArbitrAI had to navigate these differences when assessing whether TechWorks had violated IP rights by delivering software that allegedly did not meet contractual standards. German IP law, guided by EU directives, has stringent requirements for the protection of proprietary technology, while U.S. law allows for more flexibility in certain aspects of software licensing and performance guarantees.

3. Dispute Resolution Mechanisms:

Arbitration procedures also differ between the U.S. and Germany. The U.S. system typically involves more flexible discovery processes and broader judicial review, while Germany's system emphasizes efficiency and minimal court intervention. ArbitrAI's predictive analysis considered these procedural differences when estimating the likely outcomes of arbitration proceedings in each country.

Challenges and Ethical Considerations

Despite the efficiency and accuracy offered by ArbitrAI, the use of AI in international arbitration raises several ethical and procedural challenges:

1. Data Privacy and Security

Given that sensitive corporate data, including proprietary software details and financial records, was processed by the AI platform, data security was a significant concern. InfiniTech, in particular, worried that its proprietary technology could be exposed or misused during the AI analysis process. To address these concerns, ArbitrAI employed robust encryption and data anonymization techniques to protect the confidentiality of both parties.

2. Algorithmic Transparency

Similar to other AI systems, ArbitrAI operates on algorithms that are not fully transparent to the users. While the system provided valuable recommendations, there were concerns about the "black box" nature of its decision-making process. Legal professionals on both sides requested explanations for some of the AI's predictions and recommendations, emphasizing the need for greater transparency in AI-driven legal tools.

3. Bias in Legal Precedents

Another challenge is the potential bias in the AI's recommendations, which are based on historical legal precedents. If past arbitration decisions disproportionately favored certain types of companies or industries, there is a risk that the AI could perpetuate these biases. In this case, ArbitrAI relied on a broad database of international arbitration cases, ensuring a balanced approach, but the issue of bias remains a concern in broader applications.

Outcome and Impact

Thanks to the AI-powered arbitration process, TechWorks and InfiniTech reached a resolution within four months, significantly faster than traditional arbitration, which often drags on for years. The final settlement involved partial payment to TechWorks, the establishment of an escrow account, and the involvement of an independent expert to assess the software. Both companies avoided a lengthy court battle and were able to preserve their business relationship.

The successful use of ArbitrAI in this case highlights the growing role of AI in international arbitration, particularly for complex cross-border disputes involving multiple legal frameworks. By providing legal analysis, predicting outcomes, and facilitating settlement negotiations, AI tools like ArbitrAI can help streamline the arbitration process, saving time and costs for all parties involved.

Conclusion

The dispute between TechWorks Inc. and InfiniTech Ltd. highlights how AI, specifically ArbitrAI, can streamline and facilitate international arbitration in complex cross-border legal cases. By utilizing AI-driven tools, both parties were able to overcome the challenges of navigating multiple legal frameworks, including U.S. contract law, German commercial codes, and international intellectual property regulations. ArbitrAI's ability to quickly analyze vast amounts of legal data across different jurisdictions allowed it to provide accurate legal assessments, identify potential breaches, and suggest reasonable settlement options.

The use of AI led to significant time and cost savings for both companies, enabling them to avoid prolonged litigation while maintaining their business relationship. Moreover, the AI-driven approach ensured that both U.S. and German legal standards were respected, making the final settlement robust and legally sound in both jurisdictions.

However, the case also underscored the ongoing challenges of using AI in legal processes, particularly regarding data privacy, algorithmic transparency, and the risk of reinforcing biases based on historical legal precedents. While ArbitrAI proved effective in this case, these concerns point to the need for continuous oversight, ethical safeguards, and enhancements in AI systems to ensure that they serve the broader goals of fairness and justice.

In conclusion, the successful resolution of the TechWorks-InfiniTech dispute demonstrates the growing importance of AI in international legal processes. AI tools like ArbitrAI are likely to play a central role in the future of cross-border dispute resolution, particularly in a globalized economy where legal disputes increasingly span multiple jurisdictions. By integrating AI into international arbitration, companies can expect more efficient, transparent, and data-driven resolutions, though careful attention must be given to the ethical and procedural implications of these emerging technologies.

References

1. International Chamber of Commerce (ICC). "International Arbitration."

   Information on international arbitration procedures and how disputes are resolved under ICC arbitration rules. Retrieved from ICC

2. World Intellectual Property Organization (WIPO). "Resolving Disputes in International Technology Transactions."

    This document discusses how intellectual property disputes, particularly in technology transfer agreements, are resolved in international contexts. Retrieved from WIPO

3. UNCITRAL Model Law on International Commercial Arbitration.

    The United Nations' framework for resolving cross-border commercial disputes via arbitration. Retrieved from UNCITRAL

4. SmartSettle. "How AI is Revolutionizing International Dispute Resolution."

    This article discusses the use of AI tools like ArbitrAI in facilitating international arbitration and settlement negotiations. Retrieved from SmartSettle

5. Harvard Law Review. "The Role of AI in International Arbitration: Navigating Complex Jurisdictions."

    A detailed exploration of how AI is being used to manage legal complexities in international disputes. Retrieved from Harvard Law Review

Safeguarding Client Confidentiality with AI at Harrington Law Firm

Background

In 2021, Harrington Law Firm, a medium-sized law practice specializing in corporate law, decided to integrate AI tools into its daily operations. The firm wanted to leverage the power of AI for tasks such as legal research, document review, and contract analysis. However, like many legal professionals, the firm's partners were deeply concerned about the potential risks to client confidentiality and data privacy.

Before committing to AI, Harrington Law Firm conducted a thorough risk assessment, analyzing the data privacy implications of using tools like Kira Systems (for contract analysis) and ROSS Intelligence (for legal research). Their goal was to ensure that client affidavits, legal documents, and sensitive case information would remain secure.

The Implementation Process

1. Vendor Selection and Due Diligence The firm began by selecting AI vendors that adhered to GDPR and CCPAdata protection regulations.

Harrington Law Firm's legal team worked closely with AI providers to review their privacy policies, ensuring that all data processed by the AI would remain encrypted and protected from unauthorized access. The firm also required that the AI vendors undergo regular third-party audits to verify compliance with industry standards for data protection.

2. End-to-End Encryption To address concerns about client confidentiality, the firm ensured that the AI platforms used end-to-end encryption for all data exchanges. Documents containing client-sensitive information were encrypted both in transit and at rest, making it nearly impossible for unauthorized users to access the data.

3. Data Anonymization Harrington Law Firm also took advantage of the data anonymization features offered by their AI providers. For example, when using Kira Systems to analyze contracts, the system stripped personally identifiable information (PII) from the data before processing, ensuring that even if the AI analyzed large datasets, none of the specific client details could be identified or exposed.

4. Client Consent and Transparency Harrington adopted a client-consent-first approach, informing clients about the use of AI and how their data would be protected. The firm emphasized that no sensitive information would be used without explicit client consent, and they assured clients that they could request the deletion of their data at any time.

Challenges and Solutions

One of the key challenges the firm faced during the implementation process was managing internal skepticism. Senior partners were concerned that relying on AI tools could expose the firm to unforeseen data breaches. To address these concerns, the firm instituted regular training sessions for its staff, focusing on the security measures implemented by AI vendors and the steps being taken to protect client information.

Another challenge was ensuring compliance with cross-border data protection laws, as the firm dealt with international clients. Harrington Law Firm consulted with data protection experts to ensure that AI systems complied with global data privacy standards, including ISO 27001, a widely recognized international standard for data security.

Outcome: Improved Efficiency with No Compromise on Privacy

After a six-month implementation period, Harrington Law Firm fully integrated AI into its operations. The firm experienced a 30% increase in efficiency, as routine tasks such as document review and legal research were significantly expedited. Most importantly, there were no breaches or privacy violations. Clients expressed confidence in the firm's use of AI, particularly after being reassured that their sensitive information was fully protected by encryption, anonymization, and rigorous privacy policies.

Harrington's success demonstrates that AI can be implemented in legal settings without compromising data privacy, provided that the right security protocols are in place.

Relevance to Legal AI Adoption

Harrington Law Firm's case shows that concerns about data privacy, while valid, can be addressed through careful vendor selection, client transparency, and advanced security measures. By adopting an approach that prioritizes encryption, anonymization, and client consent, legal firms can confidently integrate AI technologies without risking sensitive client information.

References

1. Kira Systems. "Data Privacy and Security in AI Contract Analysis." Retrieved from Kira Systems

2. ROSS Intelligence. "How AI Can Assist Legal Teams While Maintaining Client Confidentiality." Retrieved from ROSS Intelligence

3. General Data Protection Regulation (GDPR).

   Overview of the GDPR, an important regulation for data privacy in Europe, which applies to AI tools handling client data. Retrieved from GDPR

4. ISO 27001 Standard for Information Security.

   Information about ISO 27001 and its importance in maintaining data security in legal and other sensitive industries. Retrieved from ISO 27001

What's Next: Exploring AI in Proactive Policing in India

As this book draws to a close, it's important to reflect on the far-reaching impact of AI not only in legal frameworks but across multiple facets of society. The intersection of AI and law has revealed its potential to revolutionize how justice is delivered, but this is only one dimension of AI's influence on governance and public services. The next frontier I'm exploring lies in the domain of **proactive policing**—an area where Generative AI can play a critical role in preventing crime, maintaining public order, and safeguarding citizens.

In my forthcoming book, **"Generative AI and Proactive Policing: Shaping the Future of Law Enforcement in India,"** I will delve into how AI technologies can be deployed for **predictive policing**, identifying potential threats before they materialize, optimizing police operations, and enhancing community safety. With the complexities of India's diverse socio-political environment, overburdened law enforcement agencies, and the pressing need for crime prevention, the adoption of Generative AI in policing holds the promise of bringing **transparency, efficiency**, and **responsiveness** to law enforcement.

The book will cover key areas such as:

- **Predictive Analytics in Crime Prevention**: How AI can analyze historical crime data and societal trends to predict high-risk areas and potential criminal activity.

- **Real-Time Data Processing for Rapid Response**: Using AI to synthesize data from multiple sources—such as surveillance, social media, and public reports—to enable faster and more informed decision-making by police.

- **AI in Crowd and Riot Control**: Deploying AI to monitor and analyze real-time patterns during protests or public gatherings, helping authorities maintain public order while minimizing harm.

- **Ethical and Privacy Considerations**: Addressing the critical concerns around data privacy, ethical policing, and preventing misuse of AI tools in a democracy.

With **India's diverse population and unique challenges in law enforcement**, this book will offer insights into how technology can be adapted to local contexts while enhancing public trust and transparency in policing. Much like AI's role in law, the aim is to help Indian law enforcement agencies adopt technologies that foster **proactive, data-driven policing** in a way that respects citizen rights and upholds the principles of justice.

Stay tuned for this exciting new exploration into how Generative AI can shape the future of policing in India!

References & Acknowledgements

Chapter 1: Introduction to Generative AI in the Judiciary

1. **Vidhi Legal Policy**. "Responsible AI in the Indian Justice System: A Strategy Paper." Retrieved from Vidhi Legal Policy

2. **India AI**. "AI in Judicial Systems." Retrieved from India AI

Chapter 2: Streamlining Case Backlogs with AI

1. **National Judicial Data Grid (NJDG)**. Retrieved from NJDG

2. **ProPublica**. "Machine Bias: There's Software Used Across the Country to Predict Future Criminals." Retrieved from ProPublica

Chapter 3: AI-Assisted Legal Research

1. **ROSS Intelligence**. "AI for Legal Research." Retrieved from ROSS Intelligence

2. **CaseText**. "Using AI in Legal Research to Improve Outcomes." Retrieved from CaseText

Chapter 4: AI in Courtroom Procedures

1. **Indian Express**. "AI Transcribing Supreme Court Proceedings." Retrieved from Indian Express

2. **Press Information Bureau**. "AI in Indian Judicial System: Government Initiatives." Retrieved from PIB

Chapter 5: Drafting Legal Documents Using AI

1. **Kira Systems**. "AI-Powered Contract Review." Retrieved from <u>Kira Systems</u>

2. **LexisNexis**. "Leveraging AI to Draft Legal Documents." Retrieved from <u>LexisNexis</u>

Chapter 6: AI in Judicial Decision-Making

1. **Harvard Law Review**. "AI and Judicial Decision-Making: An Overview." Retrieved from <u>Harvard Law Review</u>

2. **Ethics in AI**. "Ethical Challenges in AI-Assisted Judicial Decisions." Retrieved from <u>Ethics in AI</u>

Chapter 7: Public Access to Legal Services Through AI

1. **Law Society of England and Wales**. "AI and Access to Justice." Retrieved from Law Society

2. **LegalZoom**. "AI-Driven Legal Services: Improving Access to Justice." Retrieved from <u>LegalZoom</u>

Chapter 8: Ethical Considerations in AI-Driven Justice

1. **ProPublica**. "Bias in AI-Driven Risk Assessment Tools." Retrieved from <u>ProPublica</u>

2. **Electronic Frontier Foundation (EFF)**. "The Ethics of AI in Law." Retrieved from <u>EFF</u>

Chapter 9: AI Success Stories in Indian Courts

1. **Indian Courts E-Committee**. "Case Study: AI Implementation in Indian High Courts." Retrieved from <u>Indian Courts E-Committee</u>

2. **The Guardian**. "AI in the Judiciary: Success Stories and Lessons Learned." Retrieved from <u>The Guardian</u>

Chapter 10: Roadmap for AI Adoption in the Indian Judiciary

1. **Supreme Court of India**. "E-Courts Project: Modernizing the Judiciary with Technology." Retrieved from Supreme Court

2. **e-Estonia**. "Lessons from Estonia's Digital Court System." Retrieved from <u>e-Estonia</u>

Chapter 11: Future Trends in AI for Law

1. **McKinsey & Company**. "The Future of AI in Legal Services." Retrieved from <u>McKinsey</u>

2. **Stanford Law Review**. "AI and the Future of Law: A Long-Term Outlook." Retrieved from <u>Stanford Law Review</u>

Chapter 12: Data Privacy in Legal AI – Myths, Realities, and Adoption

1. **General Data Protection Regulation (GDPR)**. "Overview of GDPR for Data Privacy." Retrieved from <u>GDPR</u>

2. **ISO 27001**. "Information Security Standards for AI Systems." Retrieved from ISO

3. **Kira Systems**. "Ensuring Data Privacy in AI-Powered Legal Tools." Retrieved from <u>Kira Systems</u>

4. **LegalMation**. "Data Security in AI-Driven Legal Solutions." Retrieved from <u>LegalMation</u>

Acknowledgments

This book has drawn on a wealth of knowledge and resources from various experts, organizations, and publications in the fields of AI, law, and data privacy. Special thanks are extended to the following:

- **Vidhi Legal Policy** and **India AI** for providing critical insights into the application of AI in the Indian judicial system.

- **ProPublica** and **Electronic Frontier Foundation** for their investigative work on AI bias and ethical considerations.

- **ROSS Intelligence, Kira Systems**, and **LexisNexis** for their pioneering efforts in AI-powered legal research and document drafting.

- **Harvard Law Review, Stanford Law Review**, and **McKinsey & Company** for their forward-looking analysis on AI's future in law.

- **The Supreme Court of India** and the **E-Courts Project** for advancing technological adoption in Indian courts, serving as inspiration for the AI-driven reforms discussed in this book.

- **ISO** and **GDPR** authorities for their guidelines and regulations on data privacy, helping to shape the legal profession's approach to AI.

About the Authors

Aspire K Swaminathan

Aspire K Swaminathan is a visionary **serial entrepreneur** and **business strategist**, with over two decades of experience spanning various industries, including **education, technology, governance, and political strategy**. He has successfully launched and led multiple ventures, driven by his passion for innovation and his commitment to empowering others through knowledge and technology.

An **alumnus of IIM Bangalore**, Swaminathan is renowned for his pioneering work in blending technology with traditional sectors to create transformational change. Over the years, he has established himself as a key figure in leveraging **AI, data analytics**, and **generative technologies** to solve complex challenges, including his groundbreaking initiatives in **education technology** and **political consulting**.

In his entrepreneurial journey, Swaminathan has founded companies like **Aspire Knowledge Ventures**, where his focus has been on building solutions that make **AI** and **data-driven insights** accessible to a broader audience. He has a proven track record of incubating and scaling businesses that are centered on the use of **Generative AI**, in domains like Enterprise Software Solutions, Healthcare, Edtech, legal frameworks, governance, and business consulting.

Swaminathan's expertise extends beyond entrepreneurship into the realm of **governance and legal technology**. His ongoing **Doctoral Studies in Generative AI** at **Golden Gate University, San Francisco**, highlight his deep commitment to exploring the role of AI in reshaping the future. In collaboration with his co-author **Ms. Anita Thomas**, Swaminathan has crafted **"Generative AI in the Courtroom: A Practical Handbook for Modern Justice,"** a book that seeks to bridge the gap between AI advancements and the Indian judiciary.

With a deep understanding of both **technological innovation** and **legal frameworks**, Swaminathan envisions a future where **Generative AI** becomes a driving force in modernizing the judicial system, making it more efficient, transparent, and accessible to all. Through this book, he provides a practical guide for legal professionals and policymakers, empowering them to harness the transformative potential of AI for the betterment of society.

Anita Thomas

Anita Thomas is a highly respected lawyer with over **31 years of standing at the bar.** Born on **March 23, 1970,** in Chennai to **Late C. Jose Ukkur,** a Senior Advocate, and **Irene Jose,** a homemaker, Anita followed in her father's footsteps, carrying forward his legacy in law. She completed her schooling at **Good Shepherd Convent, Chennai,** and went on to obtain her **Bachelor of Law** from **Madras Law College** (now **Dr. Ambedkar Government Law College**). She also holds an **M.A. in Public Administration** from **Madras University.**

Anita's legal practice spans a wide array of specializations, primarily focusing on **Civil Law,** which encompasses a broad spectrum of corporate and individual legal needs. She is highly regarded for her work in **Maritime Law,** where she represents companies in the shipping industry, as well as her expertise in **Trademark Law, Consumer Law, Testamentary and Succession Law,** and **Corporate Law.** Her clientele includes both corporations and private individuals, with her legal services extending from **drafting agreements** and **contracts** to representing clients in **money suits, cheque dishonour cases,** and **due diligence for property matters.**

In addition to her private practice, Anita is associated with a **Cochin-based law firm,** specializing in **Maritime Law.** She is known for her strong courtroom presence, articulate arguments, and her ability to build rapport with clients, which helps them feel at ease while navigating complex legal matters. Her dedication to **honesty and integrity** remains at the core of her practice, ensuring that her clients receive justice through ethical and straightforward legal representation.

Beyond her legal practice, Anita is deeply committed to community service. She is on the **Board of Women's Christian College,** serves as a **Council Member of the Union Christian Association,** and contributes to the **Legal Affairs Committee** of the **Chennai-Bangalore Diocese of the Mar Thoma Syrian Church.** Additionally, Anita finds great joy in teaching Sunday School at the **Madras Mar Thoma Syrian Church,** where she worships with her family.

Anita is married to **Thomas A. Thomas,** who runs a public relations company. They have two children: their son, a lawyer, and their daughter, a social worker. Anita's dedication to both her legal career and community service highlights her multifaceted approach to making meaningful contributions to both her profession and society.